More Praise for Victori

". . . a true pioneer [who] will help every reader."
—Mike Dooley, *New York Times* best-selling author of
Notes from the Universe

"In a world of so many lost souls, [Victoria Price] points the way to true north."
—Parker J. Palmer, author of *On the Brink of Everything*

"Victoria Price forges an intimate friendship with her true self. This leads to a life overflowing with grace and humor, with deep darkness and sweet surprise. And we get to be the beneficiaries."
—Mirabai Starr, author of *Caravan of No Despair*

"Victoria Price shows us . . . how to face down our fears to find those happy true selves who have been waiting unseen inside us for gosh knows how long."
—Anneli Rufus, author of *Unworthy*

"In her inspiring memoir, *The Way of Being Lost*, Victoria Price walks us all back home. A must-read for anyone who dares to live a life of joy."
—Rebecca Campbell, best-selling author of
Light Is the New Black

"*The Way of Being Lost* takes us on the most exquisite journey that one can take—the road home to one's true self . . . told through the particular lens of the author's life. Though it takes great courage to make this trip, the rewards are beyond measure. And in the case of *The Way of Being Lost*, the journey is beautifully told, universally relevant, and deeply meaningful."
—Christiane Northrup, MD, *New York Times*
best-selling author of *Goddesses Never Age*

"I think when we wake up in the morning, we can choose between fear and love. Every morning. And every morning, if you choose one, that doesn't define you until the end. . . . The way you end your story is important. It's important that we choose love over fear, because love is the answer."

—Guillermo del Toro,
Oscar-winning director
of *The Shape of Water*

LIVING LOVE

12 Heart-Centered Practices to Transform Your Life

Victoria Price

ixia
PRESS

Mineola, New York

Copyright

Bibliographical Note

Living Love: 12 Heart-Centered Practices to Transform Your Life is a new work, first published by Ixia Press in 2020. Victoria Price's photo on page 155 is by Chaz Mottinger/Indiana University Cinema.

Library of Congress Cataloging-in-Publication Data

Names: Price, Victoria, 1962 April 22– author.
Title: Living love : 12 heart-centered practices to transform your life / Victoria Price.
Description: Mineola : Ixia Press, 2020. | Summary: "In this spiritual self-help book, Victoria Price encourages the embrace of the healing power of Love. From creating a daily routine of joy and gratitude to developing a practice of presence and forgiveness, she teaches that by allowing Love to work through us, we will find our true selves and become a force for transformation-not just in our lives but also in the wider world"— Provided by publisher.
Identifiers: LCCN 2019037904 | ISBN 9780486840109 (trade paperback)
Subjects: LCSH: Love. | Gratitude. | Self-perception. | Twelve-step programs.
Classification: LCC BF575.L8 P745 2020 | DDC 177/.7—dc23
LC record available at https://lccn.loc.gov/2019037904

Ixia Press
An imprint of Dover Publications, Inc.

Manufactured in the United States by LSC Communications
84010701
www.doverpublications.com/ixiapress

2 4 6 8 10 9 7 5 3 1

2020

CONTENTS

INTRODUCTION

Aʟʟ Yoᴜ Nᴇᴇᴅ
ɪs Lᴏᴠᴇ

Where Is Love?

When I was six years old, my parents took me to see *Oliver!* It was my first movie musical, and OMG! I adored everything about it: the singing, the dancing, the costumes, the sets, the story, the songs.

But there was one scene in particular that I never forgot: when Oliver, all alone in the dark basement of that lonely London orphanage, sang "Where Is Love?" in his beautiful soprano little boy's voice. His song cracked open my heart.

Even as a very young girl, I got it—though I certainly wouldn't have been able to articulate it in these grown-up words: Oliver's plaintive plea was the impetus for everything that happened, not just to him but to everyone in that movie. An orphaned boy desperately missing his mother— trying to believe that somehow, against all odds, he will find love, family, connection, safety, and hope—enters a whole world of people also looking for love wherever they can find it too.

Seeing that movie and hearing that song wasn't the first time I understood there were people in the world who didn't lead the incredibly privileged life I did. I grew up watching TV reports about the death and destruction of the Vietnam War, the hatred and hope of the civil rights movement. The nightly news brought heartbreaking images of starving children in Africa into our living room. Their anguished faces, their distended bellies, and their mouths encrusted with flies shook me to my core. Oliver's made-up movie misery couldn't hold a candle to what I saw every night on television.

My parents wanted me to know what a remarkable life I'd been given as the daughter of a movie star living in a mansion in sunny Southern California, so they didn't try to shelter me. But they weren't trying to scare me either. From the time I was a little girl, I understood that with privilege comes a responsibility to give something back to other people and to our planet. That was how they lived their lives, and it was how they wanted me to live mine.

What got to me about that song was understanding for the first time that no matter what a person's story or circumstances might be, every single being in the world wants the same thing: *to love and to be loved.*

For over fifty years now, the words of that song have sung themselves through my mind and heart over and over again. They have been a leitmotif of my life. Little did I know as a six-year-old sitting between my parents in a movie theater that the question posed in that song would become the impetus for my lifelong spiritual journey: *Where Is Love?*

What Is Love?

I never have stopped believing that we all want to love and to be loved. Yet my life has been filled with the same confusion and pain that most of us have felt: if we want to love and to feel loved, then why is it so hard? Why do we hurt others, and why do others hurt us? And if it *is* so hard, why do we care so much about loving and being loved?

I asked myself these questions repeatedly. Yet I never seemed to find answers until I stumbled upon the transformational power of heart-centered practices. Then my whole life changed, including my understanding of what Love is, what Love does, and why Love matters. This is because I became less worried about being loved and more eager, willing, and able to live in Love. Love with the Big L, that is.

What is this Love?

The Sufi poet Jalal ad-Din Muhammad Rumi lived eight hundred years ago—and he's the best-selling poet of the twenty-first century! Just as *Oliver!* gave me my first glimpse at our human longing for love, Rumi has shown me how our myriad messy and marvelous manifestations of human love can illuminate our spiritual journey to understand and live in Love.

Introduction

Among Rumi's many poems, there is one that is the most quoted. It contains everything any of us need to know about Love. In fact, it may be the greatest Love poem ever written. But this is the part that everyone remembers:

Out beyond ideas of wrongdoing and right-doing,
there is a field. I will meet you there.
When the soul lies down in that grass,
the world is too full to talk about.
Ideas, language, even the phrase "each other"
does not make any sense.

This place, this field—out beyond ideas of wrongdoing and right-doing—is Love.

In this field, we remember that Love is the essence of all existence.

We are all always drawn to this Field of Love, because it's the one place where everything feels fundamentally true and pure and safe and whole and free.

Living and loving in this field, we move beyond the limitations of our little lives into a place of oneness. The oneness of Love.

There we remember at last that Love is where we come from and where we're all ultimately going . . . but it's also where we all live, right here and right now.

And there we know beyond a shadow of a doubt that loving most certainly is what we are all here to do—just as we also know that Love ultimately has nothing whatsoever to do with "doing" at all.

Finding Love

I have spent a lot of my life looking for love, all the while loving not too wisely or too well. In fact, for a long time I felt that loving was what I had done the worst. (Though not for lack of trying!) Yet, paradoxically, even as I failed again and again at my human agenda of loving and being loved, deep down I always believed in the power of Love.

I learned in Sunday school that God is Love and Love is All. I also was taught that Love always casts out fear, that Love can heal anything. I saw it happen! I witnessed it in my own life and in the lives of others. I felt that Love. I lived in that Love as a little girl. It's just that, as I grew up, the translation of that Love into my own life felt flawed. Yet I never stopped believing that the Field of Love existed. It just seemed like I'd been condemned to spend my life trying and failing to find my way there.

Then I hit a bottom—a place that was about as low as I could go; a place from which I never would learn to love myself, love anyone else, love my life, do anything lovable. I'd been alive for almost five decades, and I felt as though I never had even shown up to my own life, let alone ever really loved. I vowed to myself to change.

But then I hit that same bottom again. And again. And again. Until, finally, just like Oliver, hopeless and alone in the dark basement, I cried out: "Where is Love?" When I felt that deep longing for Love with every fiber of my being, I finally turned to Love with my whole heart. Only then was I finally able to listen to what Love wanted me to hear.

And did I ever hear it! Loud and clear.

Now when I say "loud and clear," I don't mean it in some Charlton-Heston-as-God-speaking-from-the-sky kind of way. There was no burning bush either. Though I'd be less than honest if I didn't admit to having hoped for some kind of sign like that over the years: telling me what to do with my life and how to do it. No. I heard it in my heart, which is what usually happens when I really know what I need to do.

It goes like this: when an idea comes from Love, I feel it before I can articulate it. Next come the words, like the translation of that idea into clear directions. Then—and this is the kicker—the whole thing clicks into place in my heart like a gear settling into position or a combination lock hitting its final number. When that happens, I feel a sense of immense peace and everything inside me eases. This is how I always know that I am listening to Love.

That's exactly what happened. After years of trying to change my life, I felt the absolute peace of knowing what to do.

There was only one small problem: I didn't know *how* to do it.

Still . . . if I was desperate enough to listen, I was desperate enough to try.

What came to me was this: *create a daily practice of joy.*

But what did that even mean? I had no earthly idea! I just knew I had to find out. So the first thing I did was read everything I could about "practice" and distill it to its essence. I decided that practice entailed *doing* something—as opposed to just thinking about it—and then doing that something in a conscious, committed, daily, and deliberate way.

Okay.

The next thing I needed to know was what "joy" meant. I knew what joy *felt* like. But how do you *practice* something you are just supposed to *feel*?

Joy Is the Pure and Simple Delight in Being Alive

When I found this definition, something in my heart sang. Wow! Just wow! How I yearned for that!

I decided that I was being asked to practice (i.e., *do!*) something every day in a conscious, committed, and deliberate way that made me feel the pure and simple delight in being alive.

So I did. Every day I took a walk, cuddled with my sweet dog, photographed colorful flowers, listened to my favorite music, binge-watched *I Love Lucy* episodes I had adored as a kid, enjoyed vibrant hummingbirds buzzing at their feeder, remembered to stop and really see the beauty of a sunset. Every day I did something, anything, that felt like joy. And then—because I'm a writer, because I love to write, and because writing always has been one of my go-to ways of healing—once a week I began blogging not only about what I had done but also about how a lot of old voices in my head had tried to stop me.

I'd written books, magazine and newspaper articles, and screenplays. But I had never really blogged. I loved blogging! Not only did it feel liberating and joyful to write whatever I wanted, however I wanted to write it, but blogging connected me with other people who also wanted to create more joy in their lives. These were people just like me, struggling through their own battles with self-loathing and self-doubt, trying to find their true purpose, and learning how to love and be loved.

Practicing joy. Writing about my practice. And sharing it with others. These three things changed my life. Truly. From that dark basement, I finally emerged into the light! I went from being someone who loathed herself (a lonely workaholic who ran herself into the ground, an unfulfilled woman in her fifties who believed she had never shown up to her own potential or to love) to becoming someone who felt grateful and at peace and who loved sharing her joy with others.

I know it sounds crazy, except that everything felt transformed. This joy practice stuff actually worked!

After an amazing year of practicing joy and sharing it with people, I began to feel as though I had discovered a magical formula. Now, if I just could understand *why* this had worked, I was pretty sure it could help others as well. I thought that if I could make my life into a kind of spiritual experiment, maybe I would be able to discover why a made-up practice had succeeded when nothing else had.

It was during this time that the twenty-fifth anniversary edition of a book I had loved when it first came out was republished: Marianne Williamson's *A Return to Love.* While rereading it, a huge lightbulb went off when I saw this: "Love is what we are born with. Fear is what we learn. The spiritual journey is the unlearning of fear and prejudices and the acceptance of love back in our hearts. Love is the essential reality and our purpose on earth. To be consciously aware of it, to experience love in ourselves and others, is the meaning of life."

I saw that this was the reason creating a daily practice of joy worked when nothing else had. My whole life, I'd been trying to fix what I saw as broken. I believed I had left the Field of Love and that it was my "job" to find it again. But when I began a daily practice of joy, I did something different. I didn't try to change a behavior, habit, or way of thinking as I had in the past. Instead, I began "living as if"—as if I were still living in the Field of Love. By doing this, I invited who I always had thought I could be back into my life. Even if it was for only twenty minutes a day, I lived as if I was the person I always had longed to be: a person overflowing with immense joy, feeling deep connection, filled to the brim with hope, expressing her creativity, connecting with others in meaningful ways, and experiencing profound peace.

For at least twenty minutes a day, I was living Love!

Before that I'd been trying to fix my problems using the same mind-set that created them: I was *afraid* that I never would feel good about myself, *afraid* that I never would be able to change my life, *afraid* that I would fail myself and others. And from that place of fear, I tried to find the ways to mend myself.

Creating a daily practice of joy and writing about it shifted me out of those lifelong fears. At long last, I remembered: *the whole meaning of life is Love.*

Love Heals

How many of us have tried to change something about ourselves that we loathe or at the very least dislike a lot? Days turn into weeks turn into years turn into decades. We try everything: quick fixes; long-term solutions; we go it alone; we find support groups. Yet sooner or later, we find ourselves back where we've started—a little wiser or a little more road-weary, but still praying/wishing/pleading for something to shift and change, hoping we finally will heal.

That was me. I had breakthroughs and breakdowns. I had lightbulb moments and periods of immense gratitude often followed by deep despair. Yet it seemed as though I always ended up cycling back and through the same old same old over and over again . . . until I discovered the power of practice and realized that healing does not come when we change a habit or a behavior.

We think: if I stop overeating, I will lose weight. If I stop overspending, I will get out of debt. If I stop working so hard, I will feel less stress.

It may work for a while, but it rarely lasts. This is because the kind of deep healing we all really seek cannot happen by changing a habit. In fact, it's the opposite.

Healing does not come from change. Change comes through healing.

Let me say that again because it's the crux of everything I've learned. Real, transformational, fundamental healing doesn't come from changing a habit or a behavior. We cannot heal from the outside in. We have to heal from the inside out. I learned this through my daily practice of joy.

My life changed because Love healed it.

Sometimes the answer we need is the answer we've known our whole lives. As a little girl, I knew that Love heals. I knew it because I experienced it. But before I began my practice of joy, I forgot how to feel the Love that had always been inside me. I had barnacled it over with fear until I could barely remember its presence. But once my joy practice reconnected me with that Love, I wanted to feel it in every area of my life. So I began trying out other heart-centered practices.

The same thing happened! Old fears melted away. Ancient stories lost their grip on me. I felt hope and experienced healing as never before! Why? Because all my practices had one thing in common: *they were heart-centered practices that caused me to live as if I were living in, as, from, and through Love.* The way I had when I was a very little girl. The way I had when I knew that Love healed.

I discovered the power of living as if Love runs the show (which, of course, Love does!). When I began living Love, Love transformed my life.

Since then, I have witnessed, in awe and wonder, gratitude and joy, the transformation that choosing to practice Love every day can bring. And not just in my life, but in the lives of others. This is why I have dedicated myself to becoming a Love practitioner, creating, deepening, expanding, and sharing heart-centered practices.

This is a beautifully intuitive process. All it takes is an open heart, a desire for transformation, and a willingness to show up and practice Love. When we do, every single one of us will remember and demonstrate what we always have known in our hearts: we are all living Love.

LIVING
LOVE

MOVING FROM PROBLEM TO PRACTICE

At the end of every year, most of us make a list of New Year's resolutions.

Coming out of the holiday season, having overeaten at parties and overspent on gifts, can feel like the perfect time to think about what we want to do better as we face the beautiful blank slate of a brand-new year.

According to *Inc.* magazine, not only do we make resolutions, but we also make the *same* resolutions: dieting or eating healthier, exercising, losing weight, saving more and spending less, quitting smoking, reading more, drinking less, and finding a new job.

When you look at that list, what do you see? Probably a few things you've wanted to do yourself. I certainly do! But what I also see is precisely what makes New Year's resolutions notoriously unreliable. So unreliable, in fact, that studies have shown that although 60 percent of us make resolutions every year, less than 8 percent of us achieve them! (That doesn't stop us though. Next year we'll start all over again, determined to believe that this time it will be different.)

What I see when I look at that list is mostly fear.

Every single choice we make every single day comes down to fear or Love. Which one we choose determines our experience and our outcome in every area of our lives. Too often when we make resolutions, we are making them from a place of fear, even though it may not feel that way. Fear is the reason why resolutions usually fail.

I'm going to repeat what I just wrote because understanding this is the key to pretty much everything: *Every day we choose between fear and Love in all that we do or say or feel.* When we were little, choosing Love came naturally. You can see it in the laughing, smiling faces of kids. Even children who are challenged by illness, poverty, or abuse find their way back to joy far more easily than adults who seem to have "everything." As we get older, however, our choices become more fear-based—even choices to be or do "better." This is because we are bombarded by fear-based messages everywhere we go. We've been hearing them our whole lives, from our parents and our peers, our teachers and the media. Fear-based stories were implanted in all of us, passed down from generation to generation often in unconscious ways.

The fears that feel the most real—and therefore the most insidious and hard to identify—are the fears that came into our lives disguised as loving advice: "I am telling you this for

2

your own good. To make you a better person. To help you out in the long run." Those often go in deep and take firm root so that, slowly but surely, we begin to lose our easy reliance on the Love we felt and expressed so freely as children.

By the time we get to the point of making resolutions, fear has been driving the bus for a very long time—sometimes in very subtle ways. For example, when we say that we want to stop overeating or overspending or overindulging, when we say we want a better job or improved habits, what we usually mean is something is missing from our lives: health, money, fitness, balance, peace of mind. Which is to say, we start from a place of lack.

Lack is one of fear's fundamental tactics. It keeps us focused on our worry about what we are living without, on our anxiety about what we do not have enough of, and on our agitation about what we have lost. Even if we say "I want to eat healthier," what we're really saying underneath that positive intention is we're afraid we're not healthy.

When we start from what we're afraid is missing and then go around trying to find that, we usually start by changing our habits. What we don't see is that any time we're trying to "fix a problem," we're destined to remain stuck in the same mind-set that created it.

The mind-set that creates every problem is fear.
The mind-set that heals every problem is Love.

When we start with a problem, we've chosen fear, which means that fear will keep choosing us. When we start with a practice, however, we are choosing Love. By practicing Love, we begin living Love. That is why practice works when resolutions rarely do.

Write This Down

Remember when I said that transformation happens when we start doing something instead of just talking about doing something? Well, there's something I would like you to do right now.

I want you to pull out a blank sheet of paper (*not* in a notebook) and write this at the top in capital letters: *THINGS I WANT TO CHANGE IN MY LIFE.*

Now I'm going to ask you to make a list of anything and everything in your life that you'd like to change. But before you do, there are a few things you need to know:

- ❧ This is only for you. No one else will see it.
- ❧ There is no right way to approach this.
- ❧ This isn't etched in stone, and it's not a list that has to last forever.

Start writing down the things you wish were different *right now*. These can be big things or little things. Things you dislike and would like to dump, or something (or perhaps someone) you wish was not exactly the way it is. Approach this list any way you like, but if you need some ideas, here are a few:

- ❧ If you're someone who makes New Year's resolutions, start there. Every year, what do you vow to change? Write those down.

🐚 If you're someone who has given a lot of thought to your big issues, write those down. The big issues are those areas that have felt most immune to change. The superbugs of our souls—resistant to every known cure—are usually what we desire to change the most.

🐚 Or you can try the "My Old Stories Approach." Ask yourself what stories you find yourself telling over and over again: *After my parents got divorced. . . . My teacher said. . . . Every relationship I have been in has. . . .* See what comes up for you.

It doesn't matter where you start, because ultimately everything circles back. Big issues such as money, health, love, purpose, happiness, freedom, peace, joy, balance, fulfillment, confidence, stability, passion get translated into resolutions like spending less, creating a budget, eating more consciously, being less judgmental, getting rid of the idea that there are things we do not deserve. And all of those usually come from some old stories we've been listening to since time immemorial.

Some of us have our big issues at the tip of our tongue; some of us keep telling our old stories ad nauseam; some of us prefer to focus on what we hope will change in our lives. Most of us do and think and feel all these. Whatever approach you take, just write down anything and everything that you want to change in your life right now.

Then, when you feel like you've emptied everything inside you on to paper, here's what I want you to do:

ꙮ Put what you've written in an envelope.

ꙮ Write *THINGS I WANT TO CHANGE* on the outside.

Then rip, shred, burn, destroy the whole darn thing. Get rid of it!

Because this is NOT where our journey together starts.

You see, what I've just asked you to do is what most of us have done our whole lives: identify our problems so that we can start from there and try to fix them.

Now it's time for a whole new approach!

The heart-centered approach of living Love.

Learning from Love

This little book is all about Love.

After experiencing the transformational power of heart-centered practices in my own life, I began sharing them with friends, colleagues, and clients. I watched Love transform their lives too. Now I've gathered those same heart-centered Love practices here so that you can incorporate them into your life.

The practices are all very simple. They are made up of tools and exercises, guidelines and suggestions—so that you, too, can begin living Love in daily, deliberate, conscious, and committed ways.

In the coming chapters, we'll explore these practices together. Take your time with them. They aren't meant to be rushed through or done all at once. The practice of living Love is a lifelong process. There are no prizes for finishing first or being best. We all end up at the same place we all began: in Love.

Use this book to help you remember the power of Love in your own life. Dive in, try each writing prompt, tool, exercise, or practice at least three times. If one doesn't resonate for you right now, put it aside and focus on the ones that do. One day you may be drawn back to a discarded or overlooked practice, just as one day you may set aside a favorite for a while. This is the nature of heart-centered practice. It is fluid because it is guided by Love.

If you get an idea for a new practice you want to try, go for it! *Living Love* isn't a bible. It's a template to lay the foundation for you to cocreate your own Love-centered life (cocreated with Love and with a growing community of heart-centered practitioners). In other words, this is *your* book to do with what it you will.

But I do have one suggestion: whatever you do, invite Love in to do it *with* you, *through* you, *as* you. This is a book that Love has made, and by living Love, you will remember the you that Love has made too!

Who Do You Think You Are?

If you are anything like me, the answer to that question might not always be so pretty. If you are anything like me, you might even hear that question in a tone that sounds suspiciously like your least favorite teacher or your disapproving parent or your mean-spirited sibling. Well, guess what? It's time to turn that question on its ear. Which means this is where we are going to start our Love journey together. And you need some supplies!

So before we get going, I want you to find a notebook and a pen you love. If you're more the digital type, you can do this on your tablet. Whatever you choose, I hope that each time you look at your virtual or paper notebook, it makes you smile. Once you have got your notebook and pen or stylus, you are ready!

Throughout this book, as I share the tools that will help shape your heart-centered life, I would suggest that when you get to each new exercise or writing prompt or practice, read it all the way through in order to familiarize yourself with it, before you actually start it. After that, you can dive in.

This is your first one.

Write This Down

Who do you think you are?

That is what I want you to write on the first clean sheet of the first page of your notebook. And then stop. Seriously. Stop.

Put down your pen or stylus, and take a deep, deep, deep breath. Place your feet on the ground so that you can feel them, sit up straight, and take another deep, deep breath. Keep doing this. Keep taking deep breaths until you feel like you are present in your body and calm in your spirit. Because before we go any further together, I need you to make me a promise.

On this first clean piece of paper, promise me that you will not write anything negative about yourself. (Warning: this may be harder than it seems, and you may have to rip out a few pieces of paper or use that handy digital eraser on your tablet.) But a promise is a promise, and I need you to make me this one: *I will not write anything negative about myself.*

Write that down. I mean it! Your paper should look like this so far:

Who do you think you are?
I promise I will not write anything negative about myself.

Take a few more deep breaths. Then get ready. Because now I'm going to ask you to write down everything you love about yourself.

Yes, seriously. I want you to write down every single thing you love about yourself.

Ideally, this should feel like Christmas or the last day of school or like you've been waiting your whole life for this moment! But let's face it. For most of us, loving ourselves doesn't come easily, because we've been trained to be far more comfortable finding our own faults than tooting our own horns.

That is why we are doing this.

So if you're rolling your eyes or clenching your teeth, I get it! And if you've already fled the room, planning never to return, when you do come back and gingerly pick up this book, please hear this: I'm with you. I used to *loathe* doing things like this, and it's still not entirely in my wheelhouse. That's why I'm asking you to hang in here long enough, so you can find out *why* you despise being asked to share what you love about yourself. And to do that, you have to try this. You have to write down every single thing you love about yourself.

If you get stumped or it's a ridiculously short list, try thinking about things your family or friends have told you they love about you. Do you believe them? At least sometimes? Then write down those things. Write anything, even if it's "I have nice eyelashes" or "My dog likes me." Just write until you are done writing and nothing else surfaces. If that's one word, it's one word. If you write all day long, yay you!

Then, for the next few hours or days, I want you to allow that same question to circle through your mind and into your heart: *Who do you think you are?* If you hear anything that's not positive, if you hear any back talk (things like *Seriously, I am supposed to* love *myself?*), acknowledge it, but don't stay stuck there. Say to yourself, "I hear you, but just for today, I am not listening!" If you find yourself thinking, *This is stupid* . . . say to yourself, "Okay. This really does seem stupid right now." Then let that go too.

But if you hear something nice about yourself, something that you or others love about yourself, do pay attention. Jot it down or tell Siri or Alexa to put it in your reminders.

Keep doing this: acknowledge the negativity and then toss it aside. Only hold on to the good stuff. The stuff that comes from Love.

Then, before you go to sleep, pull out your notebook.

First, read through what you initially wrote.

Next, add in the other good stuff that circled up.

Last, read through everything you have written down one more time, and as you fall asleep, let all those things that come from Love circle through your soul. Allow yourself to feel that Love.

Finally, give yourself a big high five. Because you, my friend, have begun living Love.

A New Way

Our journey together has now begun in Love. In writing down what you love about yourself, I asked you to dive deep, past lifelong fear-based habits of self-doubt and deprecation. I asked you to choose to listen to Love. And you did it! Now I'm going to ask you to keep listening to Love. Because in order to invite the transformational power of Love practices into our hearts and lives, we have to start out where we want to end up: and that's always in Love.

As you move through the exercises and practices in this book, you may notice different kinds of feelings start to surface. If they feel unfamiliar, uncomfortable, or just plain weird, please don't worry! This is all part of learning to live as if you've never left the Field of Love. But however discomforting this living as if may feel at first, it's totally normal. You're starting to shift really old habits of being. The good news is that the more you *live as if,* the less "as if " it will feel—and the more it will feel like living!

What we're doing at the beginning of our journey together is relearning to see ourselves through the eyes of Love. Many of us didn't grow up being taught to see ourselves this way. Some of us forgot how as we grew older. This is why we need to be retaught—retaught by Love, that is. By inviting this conversation with Love back into our lives, we will inevitably begin to feel Love loving us back whole. It's a powerful feeling! But it is also one that can easily slip away at first as we move back into our busy everyday lives. That's why we need different kinds of tools and practices to help us stay centered in our hearts.

So now that we have invited Love back into our lives, our next step will be to live as if we have arrived at the place where we have been longing to go in our most heartfelt dreams and desires. But instead of viewing that as some unreachable goal or pipe dream, we're going to learn how to discover its presence in our hearts right now. In other words, instead of identifying a problem we want to fix and working our way toward its repair, our hearts will reveal the Love that heals by showing us that this Love is already inside each and every one of us.

Usually when we identify a problem that needs fixing, we find a resource that can help us: a plumber figures out what's clogging the pipes; a therapist attempts to get to the root issue; a doctor tries to identify the source of the pain; a diet outlines a new way of eating. There's nothing wrong with that approach, except that identifying the core issue sometimes doesn't help us release it. Finding the source of the pain doesn't always lead to healthy ways of relieving it. And dieting doesn't always squelch the urge to overeat. This fix-the-problem approach may be why so many of us find ourselves increasingly depressed, obese, overmedicated, indebted, and unhappy. When trying to fix the problem doesn't actually fix the problem, we can find it hard to believe that there is any way that things will ever change. We can become caught in a cycle of hopelessness and despair.

When we learn to live as if, on the other hand, we start out where we have been longing to arrive. Where's that? Well, what I learned from *Oliver!* when I was six is as true now as it was then: *Love is always where we want to go.*

So together we are going to practice Love by living Love. This means living as if we have already arrived in that place in our hearts and souls and dreams and desires to which we have been longing to go. Because when we practice Love by living Love, Love transforms our lives.

What Is Practice?

There is a famous joke that goes like this:

> *A pedestrian on 57th Street in New York City sees a musician getting out of a cab and asks, "How do you get to Carnegie Hall?" Without pause, the musician wearily replies, "Practice. Practice. Practice."*

A few years ago, I had the joy and privilege of seeing a dear friend of mine play at Carnegie Hall. Melissa Etheridge has been a professional musician for over forty years; she's won two Grammys and an Oscar and has a worldwide following. Nonetheless, playing Carnegie Hall was a big deal for her . . . as it is for all musicians. To get to play at Carnegie Hall, one of the most celebrated music venues in the world, really does take practice, practice, practice.

But does that practice have to be as wearying as that old joke implies? This is one of the questions I was excited to ask Melissa when I interviewed her for a series of articles I was writing about practice called "The Angel in the Marble."

The title was inspired by this quote from Michelangelo: *"I saw the angel in the marble and carved until I set him free."*

Applying Michelangelo's description of the art of sculpture to the art of practice was so liberating for me! It allowed me to believe that creating a daily practice of the pure and simple delight in being alive wasn't nuts.

As you become a Love practitioner, you, too, will begin to see that practice isn't what most of us were taught when we were kids. You know, doing something over and over again until we get it right. That old "practice makes perfect" thing. Sure, if you want to play at Carnegie Hall, you're probably going to have to start practicing an instrument or singing every day. And if you want to sink two winning free throws with one second left in the final game of the Final Four, you'd better start shooting a heck of a lot of free throws! What isn't true is the "right" or "perfect" part.

Practice is not about perfection. Practice is about practice, chipping away at anything that obscures our true purpose and passion in life. This is the practice of Love removing anything unlike itself. Sure, practice requires discipline, commitment, and consistency. But this doesn't mean it has to be tiresome and tedious. Because what happens when we practice is what Michelangelo experienced when he sculpted: we catch glimpses of our inner angels and begin to set them free. In other words, we liberate ourselves by practicing Love.

Melissa is one of the most dedicated practitioners I know. She plays and practices constantly to become not only a better musician but also a better performer. Yet her practice is anything but wearisome. On her most recent album, she played every single instrument—and sang! She did this because she loves making music. This is why she practices every aspect of what she loves every single day, whether it's writing a song, recording in the studio, or playing on tour.

In fact, everything she does, she views as practice. "Eventually you come to understand that it is all about the practice, not the mastery. That's because practice keeps you humble—and humility is important because it gives you a place to go. It enables you to dream the dream. And the dream is what's going to make you happy through the practicing of the dream every day. That is where the happiness lives. It doesn't lie in the materialization of the dream. It lies in the practice of it, the journey of it, every single day. Practicing helps everything. I cannot emphasize enough what a difference it makes in your life."

On Melissa's journey, however, there was one thing she never ever practiced: *she never practiced Carnegie Hall.*

Well, of course, she didn't! you're probably saying. *That's ridiculous. How could she practice Carnegie Hall?* Yet that's what so many of us do. We spend our time rehearsing in our minds what we hope our lives will look like, only to wonder why what we imagine never transpires. That's certainly what I did. I spent so much time thinking about what I wanted to do, instead of just doing it. Even worse, I was afraid I would never get to where I wanted to go that I forgot to go there at all. I twisted myself up in knots and lost the pure and simple delight in being alive!

When our journey itself is filled with purpose and passion, we can't get fooled into thinking the destination is our real goal. If Melissa had never played Carnegie Hall, her life as a musician and a person would have been filled with the same joy and meaning, because by practicing she is always living Love.

The Four Components of Practice

To fully reap the blessings of heart-centered Love practice, it helps to understand the four components of practice: *Daily. Deliberate. Conscious. Committed.*

We need to honor each and every one of these in all of our Love practices.

Daily. Studies show that whatever we prioritize in our lives not only shifts to the top of our to-do lists, but it also becomes the lens through which we experience everything. *What we make a habit becomes a habit.* If we habitually choose fear, then fear is what we will habitually feel. This is why it's important to make a daily commitment to heart-centered Love practice. *We have to make a habit of living Love.*

Deliberate. The word *deliberate* means intentional, which comes from the Latin word for "stretching." That's how I think of practice—as the stretches we must do in our souls to keep ourselves limber in Love. Fear constricts. Love expands. To deliberately practice Love every day keeps fear at bay.

Conscious. It's not enough to practice. To be conscious means to be present. If you're doing a heart-centered Love practice, but you're thinking about all the things you have to do next, then you're not present. This is why I try to check in with my heart at least three times during my practices.

Committed. This word makes so many of us nervous because it connotes pressure, obligation, duty. Try thinking of it this way instead: every day we're bombarded by fear, so if we don't commit to practicing Love, we'll slide back into fear without even knowing it. Love is reflected in the practice of Love. In other words, when we commit to Love, Love reminds us that Love has never not been committed to us!

Daily. Deliberate. Conscious. Committed. In each of your living Love practices, circle back to these descriptions and try to bring these qualities to them. When you do—when you deliberately and consciously commit to living Love every day—you won't believe how amazing it feels!

2

THE PRACTICE
OF JOY

Love Is Calling: Are You Listening?

One of the biggest obstacles of the problem-solving approach to life is that it can prevent us from hearing our own hearts. We may feel like something's missing, but we not only don't know what it is, we also don't know how to figure out what it is.

Decade after decade, I had this nagging feeling that I wasn't showing up to my own life. I felt like there was something I was being called to do and not only was I not doing it, I wasn't even sure what *it* was.

The one thing I did know was that it had something to do with sharing my spiritual journey. As Love shepherded me through illness and debilitating anxiety, disastrous breakups, and spectacular business failures, Love taught me how to face my fears and Love healed them. The more I learned about Love, the more I wanted to impart what I was learning. But I was too scared, constantly bombarded by fear's questions: *Who do you think you are? What makes you think you have anything to share? Why do you think anyone would care about your spiritual ideas?*

This same pattern played itself out constantly. I heard Love calling to me to share my journey . . . and then I let fear throw me under the bus with its constant nay-saying. As a result, I felt like I'd never shown up to my own life, let alone my own heart. This went on for a long time until, at long last, I finally became desperate enough to *truly* listen and lean on Love.

It was 2011, and I had been invited to celebrate what would have been my father's one hundredth birthday at events created by and for his fans all over the world. Everywhere I went, I was overwhelmed by a sense of how his joy had made a profound impact on everyone he had met, as well as on people who only knew him as an actor. My dad had moved through the world as a bright light. To be bathed in that light—for a minute or a lifetime, in person or on-screen—changed anyone who experienced it. My dad consciously spent every day spreading joy. To be in the presence of his joy made you feel joy. He loved life, so life loved him. To feel his love of life made you love life, too! My dad lived Love.

I grew up bathed in that light, filled with that joy and surrounded by that love of life. But little by little, fear took over, until I became a doubtful, worried workaholic, unsure of her own worth and purpose. When I began remembering my father's joy and sharing it with his fans, I remembered my own joy. My joy showed me where I needed to go: I needed to keep sharing this legacy of Love. But when all the celebrations ended, I found myself slipping right back into my old habits. I struggled to hold on to the joy I'd felt. The only difference was now I had a clue: joy was my way back to my heart. Which is why when Love told me to create a daily practice of joy, I listened. Then . . . practicing joy transformed my life!

This is why I have chosen joy as your first Love practice. *Joy is the pure and simple delight in being alive.* You get to practice that! How? Well that's the best part. You get to decide. You get to create your own joy practice.

So read the rest of this chapter before you start. When you've done that, pull out your notebook, open it up to a clean page, take out that timer, set it for ten minutes, and promise not to stop writing.

Write This Down

What brings me joy?

Then write down every single thing in your life that brings you joy or has ever brought you joy. Ever! This could be anything at all: animals, travel, ice cream, a hug, a Sunday drive, sunshine, your mom, your grandchildren, graduation, getting an *A* in statistics, horror movies, a new pair of shoes, the way your dog jumps up and squeals when you come back from a trip. You get the idea. Write it all down for ten whole minutes, even if there are some doodles and "blah blah blahs."

Then, get up, stretch your legs, have some water.

Once you've cleared your head, come back and read through what you have written. As you do, I'm going to ask you to cross out anything that does not make you feel "the pure and simple delight in being alive." *Pure* and *simple* are the operative words here. For example, if eating ice cream brings up guilt, cross it out. If buying a new pair of shoes means you can't pay the electric bill, cross that out. If binge watching horror movies until 2:00 a.m. means you'll get to work tired and possibly piss off your partner to boot, cross that out too.

What we're looking for is anything and everything that *feels* like pure and simple delight. And what I want you to do is circle those. Circle anything that makes your heart feel joy!

If you end up finding that you don't have anything to circle, don't panic. You may have been overthinking things. We all fall into this trap: writing can bring up bad memories of school papers that some teacher will read and criticize. That's not what this is about. The freewriting you're doing is just for you. Truly! And freewriting actually will help you begin to override heady habits and connect with heart-based feeling instead.

Joy comes from our hearts. So if you didn't feel much joy because you got all up in your head, just try more freewriting. Allow yourself to tap into the pure and simple delight that each and every one of us has inside our hearts. After that, go back through what you've written and see if you can find something that feels like pure and simple delight.

Don't be afraid of doing more freewriting: write until you have one or two words or phrases circled. These will become the basis for the next phase of your practice.

Percolate

Now that you have some words circled, let them begin to percolate from your head and into your heart. So go for a walk, clean your house, take a drive, meditate, dance, watch the sunset. Do whatever you need to allow what you've done to seep into your soul for a bit.

While you're percolating, let me share a few thoughts that may help ideas bubble up for you. Because if your list says "horses, sunshine, and your mom," you may be wondering how the heck you are supposed to practice those. Especially if you do not have a horse, you live in Seattle, and your mother is no longer around. Well, none of that is a deterrent. In fact, you may be surprised what will come up for you once you realize that your only goal is to show up to the pure and simple delight of horses, sunshine, and your mom.

Maybe this will inspire you: as a lifelong sports fanatic, every spring I enjoy picking my college basketball brackets as part of the Joan Chanin Memorial March Madness Challenge, created by a son to honor his mother, a woman who apparently loved sports as much as I do.

Although I never met Joan Chanin, I feel as though I know her through the stories her son, Chris, shares with us bracketeers. This past year he wrote to us: "Whether it was waving a cowbell at my brother's football games, cheering loudly 'That's my son' at my football games, my mom was always ever present. Even up to her passing, she would always put out a spread for games and then would watch, cheer, shout, and cry at all sports from the Olympics to football to auto racing! Several times a week, I would get calls from her when watching games and hear her joyfully exclaim, 'Did you see that?'"

Now, every year as I celebrate college basketball with a group of people scattered all over the United States, connected only through our joy in sports, we all imagine Joan watching and cheering on the games from beyond. If that is not a practice of joy, I don't know what is!

Joy, you see, is contagious. The joy of Chris's mom lives on in me and in every single one of us sports lovers.

That is why a daily practice of joy is transformational. A little joy goes a long way, because the moment you feel it, you can't help but share it with others. A dose every day can lift your spirits, along with the spirits of everyone you meet when you are practicing it. Joy is pure Love. So practicing joy lands us in the Field of Love, where we remember what it is to be Love, express Love, live Love, love Love.

Sound good? Trust me. It is!

Here is how I practice the pure and simple delight in being alive: I walk my dog every day. (Both walking and my dog are on my joy list.) When I do, I stop and look up at the sky. (Nature is on my joy list.) I walk with my cell phone in my pocket, and I sometimes use it to photograph something I have seen that I find beautiful. (Creativity is on my joy list too.) Sometimes I call a friend, and we "walk" together. (Friends and connection are both on my list.) Other times I listen to an audiobook. Other times I listen to music. (Reading and music are on the list.) There are moments I turn off the phone and commit to being fully present right where I am. (Presence is one of my most essential Love practices.) And, usually, I talk to the birds, the sky, to Love—and I say thank you for all the Love I feel right where I am. (Gratitude is also one of my go-to Love practices.)

I do this every single day, whether I want to or not. Because, yes, there will be days when, ridiculous as it may sound, you actually will not want to practice joy. You'll tell yourself that you are too tired, too busy, too depressed. But practice means committing to showing up to it every single day for at least twenty minutes.

YOUR PRACTICE OF JOY

Now you get to try it out for yourself. When you're ready, when you feel like a few of the words are resonating for you, it's time to create your practice by connecting to the pure and simple delight of it. Let that delight simmer until it cooks up an idea for you to try.

Do you enjoy taking the time to smell the roses? Great! Practice that.

Do you love walking at night? Wonderful! Practice that.

Do you appreciate exploring new places? Fantastic! Practice that.

You can try anything you like, as long as it brings you joy. If it doesn't, dump it.

Your guidelines are simple:
- Set aside twenty minutes a day to consciously practice joy.
- Commit to doing it every single day.
- When you're practicing joy, make your practice deliberate by being as present as possible. (Try not to check your texts or social media feed!)

Your practice is equally simple:
- Your mission is to try doing any one of the things you wrote about that brings you the pure and simple delight in being alive.
- There's no right or wrong. Just show up to what brings you joy and do it!

Love practices teach us:
- The more Love you feel, the more Love you express.
- The more Love you express, the more Love others experience.
- The more Love others experience, the more Love others express.

And that is all that creating a daily practice of joy is about. Now go out and enJOY!

3

THE PRACTICE
OF GRATITUDE

The Illusion of Fear

The more we start living Love through our practices, the more we are choosing Love. As we begin to tap into the transformative power of our heart-centered practices and start to feel the amazing flow of Love, there are times when it may seem like all we're going to need to do from now on is to keep enjoying the ride. That's true . . . until we run smack into the brick wall fear throws up in front of us. When this happens, we can feel blindsided or terrified and even angry. Even though we are consciously choosing Love and practicing it every day, fear is still getting us to buy into its agenda.

How's that possible? It's because fear is a habit, one we have been honing our whole lives. But here's the good news: all habits can be broken.

But how? This is the key: *The less afraid we are of fear, the less fearful we will be.* So in order to truly become Love practitioners, we need to learn how to look fear in the eye and then choose Love. And in order to do this, we need to understand a little more about how fear gets our ear.

Napoleon Hill, one of the first and most influential self-help gurus of the twentieth century, said that fear is nothing more than a state of mind. He was absolutely right. Our fears *are* nothing more than a state of mind. Except that when we're being dragged around the room by our fears, tossed like a rag doll in the mouth of a saber-toothed tiger, sweating through another dark night of the soul, knowing that fears are nothing more than a state of mind usually makes precious little difference.

That's precisely because fear *is* a state of mind, and so trying to assuage fear with our minds is like trying to stop a nuclear attack by deploying more nuclear weapons. It's not going to end well. Only Love can truly cast out fear, because the lens of Love allows us to recognize fear as the illusion it actually is. So the real key to kicking the habit of fear is to wake up to the power of Love. When we do, the less real fear will seem. But I wouldn't be doing you any favors if I didn't tell you this: the more we awaken, the louder fear may clamor for our attention. This can feel confusing and scary until we really understand what's happening.

That's why I want to be clear about one thing in particular: when I talk about fear, I'm actually not talking about something. *I am talking about nothing.*

- 🪷 Fear is not a boogeyman out to get us.
- 🪷 Fear is an illusion from which we one day awaken to find we never have left the Field of Love.
- 🪷 Fear is false evidence appearing real. No matter how real, how scary, or how convincing fear may feel, it is never real.

Don't believe me? Study after study has shown that most of what we fear never happens. Yet studies also show that most of us spend two hours a day worrying. Which means that by the time we turn sixty-five, we will have spent more than five years of our lives feeling anxious about events that have an 8 percent chance of ever occurring! Crazy, right? That's because, as the Irish poet and wisdom keeper John O'Donohue knew, "Fear is the greatest trickster of all. It makes what is real seem unreal, and it makes the unreal real."

Want to hear something even crazier? Despite living in what has been statistically proven to be the safest time in human history, studies show we are becoming more and more afraid. We are increasingly fearful people living on an increasingly fear-filled planet. This fear generates more fear-based acts, which, in turn, make us more afraid. So how do we break this cycle of fear? By inviting Love into our lives. Even when—especially when—we're feeling afraid. To do that, we must remember that everything begins and ends with Love.

We are all born knowing how to love. Loving isn't something we need to be taught. Being afraid, on the other hand, is a learned behavior. We learn to become fearful either by experiencing or hearing about something that makes us afraid. Fear is contagious. We catch the fear, and then we feel it. At which point rational thought goes right out the window.

Both Love and fear manifest as feelings. But they happen ass-backward. Love begins in the heart. We feel Love long before it occurs to us to quantify or understand or explain it. Fear is exactly the opposite. The heart-gripping feeling of fear begins in our heads and then courses through our bodies. Fear is a story told to us by the world; Love is the heart essence of all experience.

We need to create heart-centered Love practices that replace our habitual patterns of fear. Sound too simplistic? Stanford research scientist Alia Crum doesn't think so. Dr. Crum believes that changing our minds can absolutely change our lives: "Our minds are not passive observers simply perceiving reality. Our minds actually change reality." This means that the way we choose to experience life determines the life we live—not just today and not just for ourselves. The reality of our individual and planetary futures is a direct consequence of whether we choose Love or fear today!

The Price of Fear

In the aftermath of 9/11, my friend Karen worked for FEMA in New York City, providing free counseling services to those who had lost loved ones, to eyewitnesses who had been there when the Twin Towers came down, as well as to anyone struggling with general anxiety after that traumatic event.

It was not long before she began to notice a pattern among those who seemed to have the most difficulty working through their anxiety and stress. When Karen asked these people how often they watched the news on TV, their answer was always the same: "Oh, I always have the news on. I *have* to keep watching it."

Karen started asking these men and women of all ages to watch less of the media coverage that relentlessly replayed the scenes of that horrific day. She even asked some people whose anxiety seemed most intense to turn off the TV altogether—for a whole week! Initially, they were resistant, convinced that those news reports were their lifeline to making sense of what had happened.

Yet when they returned to talk to Karen after watching less of the news or, better yet, no news at all, their stress levels had dramatically decreased. Karen helped her clients to see that in watching the news, they were not only reliving the trauma they had experienced, but the news reports also were creating new anxiety about what might happen next. Breaking that cycle of trauma began a new cycle of healing.

Most of us have no idea how bombarded we are with fear-based messages, and not just by the media. It starts when we are babies. The fear we hear first usually comes from the people who are supposed to love us the most: our parents.

Toward the end of her life, my mother finally told me something I always had intuitively known: since before I was born, she had been afraid that something bad might happen to me. That was why she'd always kept me on such a tight leash, monitoring what I ate, where I went, who I did or didn't spend time with. Her rigorous life lessons were all aimed at keeping me "safe," and the rules and regulations she imposed were meant to prevent catastrophe.

As a little girl, I felt my mother's fear and hated it. I vowed that I never would let her fear stop me from being me. I rebelled by riding horses that threw me over fences. I gleefully dusted myself off and hopped back on, determined to never let fear win.

What I couldn't see then was that I was just pitting fear against fear: my mother's fears for me against my fear that I would end up as fearful as my mother. What I didn't know then was how easily the virus of fear infiltrates our lives, and that once it does, it infects every thought we have, which in turn affects everything we do.

By the time I was a teenager, fear had managed to worm its way into almost every area of my existence, where it constantly told me that I just needed to follow the rules and play it safe in order to feel safer in the world.

This is fear's most persuasive argument: "Are you scared? I can offer you certainty in an uncertain world."

Sure, I felt afraid. The older I got, the more there seemed to be afraid of. But I also felt ashamed of feeling afraid. So I tried to act like I was the same fearless little girl I once had been. On the outside, I looked like a rebel who stood up to the conventions of the world and was determined to "be her own person." Yet more and more I found myself seeking security in the people, places, and things that fear promised would bring me safety. These were, of course, the same people, places, and things that fear promises will bring everyone safety: the "right" relationships, schools, jobs, homes, communities, churches, doctors, meds, institutions, etc.

As Max Lucado tells us: "When fear shapes our lives, safety becomes our god. When safety becomes our god, we worship the risk-free life. . . . The fear-filled cannot love deeply [because] love is risky." This is how so many of us end up forgetting the Field of Love. This is also why it often feels safer to trust an institution or an identity than it does to trust our own hearts.

Fear is the ultimate con game, and it's played in every language, every religion, every social stratum, every country in the world. We all pay to play. We are all paying the price of fear.

Fear is also a master magician, making it seem as though being afraid is totally reasonable and so condoning whatever fear-based actions we may take. We can all see that this usually doesn't work out well. When we choose fear over Love, we live in fear. But if our mind-sets of today create our experiences of tomorrow and consciousness constructs reality, do we really want to keep choosing fear instead of living Love?

Even more important, can we afford to keep choosing fear? Fear is the root cause of all hatred, violence, and exclusion. Fear is the foundation of the ideologies that pit us against each other as well as the natural world. To dismantle fear in our individual lives has a profound trickle-down effect for our planet.

A few years ago, I read the *New York Times* best seller *Dying to Be Me*, written by a woman who had died of stage four cancer and then miraculously came back to life . . . healed! Anita Moorjani believes she was healed precisely so she could share this message with everyone who could hear it: "Love is what we are born with. Fear is what we learn. The spiritual journey is the unlearning of fear and prejudices and the acceptance of love back in our hearts. Love is the essential reality and our purpose on Earth. To be consciously aware of it, to experience love in ourselves and others, is the meaning of life."

Fear is what we learn. Now we must unlearn it. For ourselves and for our world.

We learn fear because our parents learned it and our teachers learned it and our peers learned it. We learn fear because the media and business leaders and politicians learned it. We all learned it, which means we didn't come here with it. We all learned it, which means we don't have to leave here with it.

The more we begin to see the degree to which all our lives have been built on a global foundation of fear, the more we can begin to disempower fear by dismantling that false foundation. Every day we have to choose between fear and Love. We have to be willing to let go of the old habits of thought and the old stories that we have listened to for far too long. And then, together, begin to cocreate a whole new way of being for ourselves and for our beautiful world!

The Antidote to Fear

Fortunately, for all of us, there is a heart-centered Love practice that is the best fear antidote in the world. It's called gratitude.

Gratitude is the antithesis of trying to solve a problem from the mind-set that created it. Instead of fixing something we're afraid will never change, we take stock of the Love in our lives and then move out from there. This short-circuits fear on the spot—because when we are grateful for something, we are choosing Love.

More than anything, it was my mother's influence that led me to understand the power of practicing gratitude. As fearful as my mom could be, she also moved through her life with immense gratitude for every person, every animal, every place, every experience, every gift. She taught me how powerful it is to acknowledge gratitude for our lives. But it wasn't until I discovered that gratitude was also the antidote for the ways that my mother's fears had lived on through me that her gift came full circle.

It took me years to see how the fears my mom had passed down had become ingrained into my life. I carried around some old stories for so long that they no longer even felt like stories. They seemed to have become "me."

We all have those old stories, don't we? Well, for me, every old story that hog-tied my heart was related to something my mother had said or done to me during my childhood. At the same time, I knew that she had loved me and had tried to be the best mother she could be. Some of the greatest gifts of my life had come from my mother. At some point, it began to feel absurd to keep pinning all my problems on a woman who not only was no longer alive, but who I knew also had always wanted the best for me.

I desperately needed to let those old stories go. So, having embraced a daily practice of joy inspired by my dad, I decided to begin creating a committed practice of gratitude inspired by my mom. I started with my weekly blogs, where I began to acknowledge and express gratitude for everything I had learned from her. Every time a sorry old story surfaced, I countered it with an expression of deep gratitude in a daily, deliberate, conscious, and committed way. Slowly but surely my perspective changed.

Gratitude was the heart-centered practice that removed all the "old mother baggage" I'd been carrying around for so long. I'll never forget the day I realized this. I was hiking in the Hudson River Valley one beautiful morning when suddenly the thought came to me: *Something is missing!* And I knew what it was: all the old stories. They were literally gone! As if they never had existed. All that remained in my heart and my mind was a deep and lasting feeling of love and connection for this woman, who had taught me the power of gratitude.

This experience taught me that the only way we really can change a habit of fear is if we are willing to release the compulsive old story driving that habit and begin living Love instead. That is what a committed practice of gratitude does! And now it's time to create yours.

Giving Thanks

The beauty of practice is it can take many forms. This is particularly true with gratitude. Basically, gratitude means that you are saying thank you for/to something or someone in your life. There are so many beautiful ways to express our thanks. That's precisely why I've chosen this as your second heart-centered Love practice. We get to transform one of the most heartfelt human emotions into a daily, deliberate, conscious, and committed means of living Love into every nook and cranny of your life.

Here are a few ideas to inspire you. Start playing around with them and see which ones resonate for you. Feel free to riff on these or change them up:

Gratitude Lists. Once a day, in the morning or at night—or whenever you need it if you are being bombarded by fear—write down everything for which you are grateful. It's like freewriting your thanks. Literally, write down every single thing. This immediately short-circuits any fear-based thinking that seems to have taken over and returns you back to the Field of Love.

Variation on This Theme: I have a friend who has written down three things which she's grateful for every night of every year for five years. Each time she gives thanks, she also sees what she's given thanks for in previous years. She does this before she goes to sleep, so she can always close out her day by acknowledging her own personal history of Love.

Letters to Love. I often write letters to Love, in which I offer up huge shout-outs of thanks to various people and even to experiences I've had. I address these letters to Love itself. As in *Dear Love, Thank You . . .* And I go from there. I find that when I'm feeling disconnected from my heart, this aligns me with Love in the most intimate of ways.

Thank You, World. When I'm on my morning walk, I speak my gratitude out loud. I like to say thank you to the sky or the trees or the sun. This turns a simple walk into a beautiful journey through the Field of Love. As I start out, I say to the birds and bugs and deer and even snakes I see or hear: *Good morning, all my relations. Thank you for sharing this day with me.* I also say thank you to my dog . . . or even my car. In fact, thanking inanimate objects has become one of my favorite practices of gratitude.

Variation on This Theme: I spend a lot of time on the road alone—on planes and trains, in rental cars and hotel rooms and Airbnbs. For a day or a week, these become my temporary homes. Some are nicer than others, but I always feel grateful for the shelter they provide me. So now when I take my seat on a plane or get ready to disembark, when I enter a hotel room or leave it for the last time, I say hello and I say goodbye. Then I say thank you and wish it well with its next occupant. Every time I do this, I am filled with the presence of Love, connecting me not only to right where I am, but also to those who were here before me and will come after me.

Saying Thanks. This is the most basic act of gratitude: saying thank you to everyone we encounter, from the tollbooth keeper, the busboy, the tech support person to our partner, our best friend, our boss. It's amazing how often we forget to express our gratitude to other human beings. When we do remember, the effect is profound for everyone.

Obviously, there are many ways to express gratitude. Some of the ones I've suggested may seem obvious and others downright strange. But the point is this: it doesn't matter how you do it. It matters that you do it. Be conscious of everything you're grateful for, because gratitude always connects us to Love. When we feel grateful, we are living Love. This is why it always will help shift us out of fear.

YOUR PRACTICE OF GRATITUDE

A practitioner friend once told me that anxiety is ingratitude in advance. I had to think about that for a while before I understood what she meant. I came to realize that when I'm anxious, I'm afraid of what's going to happen. If gratitude is being aware of the presence of Love, then anxiety is the denial of that presence in the future. What a waste of time to be ungrateful for something that hasn't even happened yet! But that's how fear dupes us.

Once we let future fears in the door, we stop seeing all the present good around us. That's why we practice. Gratitude is both proactive and preventative, conscious and collaborative. It always brings us back to the present as well as the presence of Love, as manifested in everything and everyone we encounter. In a world where we are often bombarded by everything that could go wrong or has gone wrong, practicing gratitude reminds us to keep choosing Love.

Here are some gratitude practice guidelines:

- ❦ Commit to spending five minutes a day consciously practicing gratitude.
- ❦ Make your practice deliberate by being as present as possible.
- ❦ Do any of the exercises described above (or one you create).
- ❦ There is no right or wrong. Just show up and be grateful.
- ❦ Acknowledge gratitude, speak gratitude, write gratitude, show gratitude.
- ❦ EnJOY gratitude!

My own gratitude practice has taught me that the more conscious we become of everything for which we are grateful and the more we acknowledge it every day, the way we experience life will shift. This is because our lives always will reflect the Love we express. So be glad, give thanks, rejoice. Live Love every single day!

4

THE PRACTICE
OF WITNESSING

Remembering Who You Really Are

B y becoming more aware of our habits of fear and coun-
teracting them with the heart-centered Love practice
of gratitude, we're setting ourselves up for our next step:
identifying the specific fears that have become the blocks
to Love in our lives. This can sometimes feel challenging
because much of the time we don't even know we're acting
out of fear.

What we do and how we think just seem like who we
are. They're not! *We are who we have learned to become. But
that isn't who we have to remain.* We just have to ferret out
the ways these old voices and their old stories have become
obstacles to the Love that is our natural state of being. We
need to learn to recognize the price each of us has paid for

listening to the world's fear disguised as our own. And then we need to stop giving fear a free ride by living Love instead, every single day.

Not only do we need to do this, we need to do this **together**! *Understanding that we are neither unique nor alone in our fears immediately begins to loosen fear's grip on our thinking.* Together we will keep creating and sharing heart-centered practices that connect us heart to heart instead of fear to fear. This is the beginning of all the healing and transformation we've been longing for—for ourselves, for our loved ones, and for the world. Together we can and will face our fears by living Love!

What Are You Most Afraid Of?

This is not a question most of us like to think about. But ignoring what scares us plays right into fear's game plan. Fear wants us to avoid talking about what we are afraid of because fear likes to keep things on the down low. *Facing our fears is the first step to eradicating them and healing our lives.* Remember, *we give fear all the life it has.* Without our cooperation, fear is nothing (which is all it has ever been anyway!).

We can face our fears together by asking ourselves one important question head-on—and then keep asking it of ourselves. So read through this next section, and then take out your journal, open to a fresh page, and get ready to write your fears away!

Write This Down

What am I most afraid of?

I journal my own answers to this question quite often, especially when fear is nattering on in my ear about something. It is always amazing to see what surfaces: old fears, new fears, and fears I didn't even know existed. But, inevitably, when I'm done writing, I feel far less fearful than when I began, as though the fear that had me so anxious had merely been floating along on the surface waiting to be swept away by Love. What inevitably surfaces through my journaling is a direction or a solution, along with a deep conviction that Love will heal whatever I seem to fear.

So now it's your turn. Set your timer for ten minutes and get ready to freewrite without stopping. Put down on paper everything that comes into your mind. No editing. And if you run out of things to say, just blather on about anything until that anything takes you to the next place you need to go.

Then, when you're done, stop for a moment. You're going to need to give yourself time to feel whatever surfaces. Take a little break. Get up and walk around. Go outside and look at the sky or the trees. Shake off whatever came up before you go back to read more.

Once you have cleared your head a little, it's time to process what arose, to dive a little deeper. In order do that, I want to share questions that you can journal about or mull over as you move through your day:

- 🐚 Did writing stir some uncomfortable stuff up for you? If so, what?
- 🐚 Did anything arise that surprised or shocked you? Write about it.
- 🐚 Was this process more or less scary than you imagined? In what ways?
- 🐚 Did you find that you were able to see beneath the fear you wrote about? Describe how that felt for you.
- 🐚 Did writing about your fears help you let any go?
- 🐚 Are you less afraid now? Try to describe how you feel.

Take your time with this process. This work we are doing is the beginning of a whole new way of being, and you need to learn how to hold your own hand. These are questions you'll return to in your freewriting—because by looking at what comes up, you are facing your fears.

Facing our fears is an ongoing process for Love practitioners. So as we move forward, it's super important to understand what can happen when we consciously face our fears. Stuff gets chemicalized. In other words, when we invite Love into unconscious places in our thinking, it's like using Drano for the soul. Love cuts through the fear that's been clogging up our lives. Old ways of thinking, being, believing, and moving through the world begin to break up and dissolve. Old stories get stirred up as they lose their hold on us.

This is actually a good thing. But it can feel uncomfortable because we've spent so many years like this. We have no idea how gunky we've become. So the dissolution of something we've believed ourselves to be can bring up feelings of disconnection, fear, anxiety, and even physical discomfort.

The key is to recognize what's happening. When the truth of Love flushes out fear, the disturbance, discomfort, and dismay we feel creates a commotion as our consciousness reawakens. Although it's nothing to be scared of, it sure can seem like it! Remember: what we are sensing is fear's fear of being replaced by Love. Knowing this can help us have the courage to keep choosing Love and living heart-centered lives.

Not Being Scared of What Scares Us

Anytime we face our fears like this, what surfaces is incredibly individual. But there is one common ground: when we begin to see the ways that fear has insinuated itself into our lives, we often become afraid that fear will never leave. We get hoodwinked into becoming afraid of fear!

In her first go at a fear-purging freewriting, my friend and colleague Rachel began by describing some of the "manageable" things she used to be afraid of, like spiders or throwing up. But she quickly dove deeper as she wrote about the kinds of fears she'd been experiencing more recently. The more she wrote, the more shocked she was to see how deeply fear had infiltrated every area of her life!

At the end of her freewriting, Rachel expressed something that so many of us feel: "What am I most afraid of? That this is who I am now. That this is my new normal. That who I was is gone forever. That God, although with me all the time and loving me all the time, might grow weary of me. And I will never be able to crawl back out of this hole I seem to have fallen into. I'm most afraid of becoming someone I don't recognize."

Although facing our fears can feel scary, it can feel even scarier to recognize the ways that fear seems to have taken up permanent residence in our souls. We worry: has the person we thought we were gone away forever? In fact, this is exactly the kind of question we need to ask ourselves—because facing our fear of fear often becomes that kick in the pants, urging us to wake up.

Fear will always try to convince us that being awake is way too scary. This is why so many of us sleepwalk through our lives. When fear becomes foundational, continually advocating for more safety nets and more illusions of control, we obligingly build them and use them. It takes guts to stop listening to fear's arguments when everyone else seems to think fear feels more normal than Love. But there is one person who knows the truth.

Meet Your True Self

"Deep down we know exactly what is going on. Deep within us is a knowing that is more sophisticated and sure than the surface patterns of our minds. But you can't reach that if you don't give yourself a chance."
—John O'Donohue, poet & theologian

Now that we're beginning to glimpse fear's modus operandi, it's time to give ourselves that chance for deep knowing. Together.

Together we're going to dive below the surface of fears that try to grab our attention and reconnect with that deep knowing with which each of us was born. This knowing comes from Love. It has never left Love. No matter how many fears have bombarded us throughout our lifetime, this deep knowing has never left us—because this deep knowing *is* us.

This deep knowing is your True Self.

Your True Self is who you are beneath everything you have learned to think, to be, to do in your life. Your True Self has never abandoned you. Your True Self has never stopped speaking to you. Your True Self has never stopped loving you. Your True Self has never stopped living Love. This is because your True Self is the only you there really is, and it has always been and always will be rooted and grounded in the Field of Love. When we begin to live as our True Selves instead of playing out our learned identities, we remember what it feels like to live in the Field of Love. (Spoiler alert: It feels incredible!)

So how do you get to know your True Self?

When you thanked yourself for facing your fears, when you let yourself feel how brave you are, when you talked to yourself about what you are afraid of, who was doing the talking? Who was doing the listening? Which one of you is your True Self?

In his best-selling book *The Untethered Soul,* Michael A. Singer teaches us how to get to know who we really are underneath the people we were taught to become. He demonstrates that "realizing that you are not the voice of the mind—you are the one who hears it" can transform our lives completely.

Most of us go through our days with a steady stream of mental chatter that we call "me." We wake up to our to-do lists, to our plans for the day, to the dramas and difficulties of our lives and our world, to the long history of who we've been day after day with our pains and pounds and people and places. But this is just who we perceive we are.

We grew up thinking what we were taught to think. We reconstituted the stories that were passed down through the centuries into individual identities with names, ID numbers, families, jobs, bodies, and histories. But those identities are only the parts we have been told to play. Meanwhile, our True Selves have been patiently waiting for us to wake up and remember who we really are. Our True Selves never have been affected by all this hoopla. Our True Selves are fearlessly grounded in Love, so in order to face our fears, we need to get better at hearing the quiet voice of Love spoken by our True Selves.

The problem is most of us listen to anything and anyone but our True Selves. The voice that I heard every day for decades more often than not beat me up with my own to-do list, kept me rehearsing past miseries, had me quaking in my boots with old fears of failure or of impending doom. That voice judged me, judged my life, judged other people's lives. That voice wore me out.

When I began learning about my True Self, I realized that voice was not me. What a relief! I had no idea how much time I spent each day eaten up by judgment and criticism. Judgment and criticism are fear-based. Which meant that I'd been spending a lot of time being afraid. We judge and criticize ourselves and others because we're afraid we are not and never will be enough.

Enough what? Enough to meet some ideal that someone planted in us long ago about what good enough is. Pretty or smart or successful or marriageable or wealthy enough. Well here's what Love knows and fear would like us to forget: *You, your True Self, is always enough.* The more you get to know your True Self, the more you'll understand that you've always been more than enough! For everyone and everything! And the more you know your True Self, the less ominous fear will seem.

That's why this next practice is so powerful. It teaches us how to turn fear away at the door, by not engaging with it. Instead of judging and criticizing ourselves and others, we learn to witness our thoughts and then let them go. Doing this as a daily, deliberate, conscious, and committed Love practice is the most beautiful way of getting to know your True Self.

Letting Go of Judgment

I learned about witnessing by reading Ram Dass, who, like Michael Singer and John O'Donohue, believes that deep inside each of us is a part of ourselves that is "aware of everything—just noticing, watching, not judging, just being present, being here now." Ram Dass suggests that we each cultivate what he calls "witness consciousness," which means learning how to look at our own lives ourselves without judging or criticizing. He writes, "Witnessing yourself is like directing the beam of a flashlight back at itself. . . . That process of stepping back takes you out of being submerged in your experiences and thoughts and sensory input and into self-awareness. Along with that self-awareness comes the subtle joy of just being here, alive, enjoying being present in this moment."

I loved this idea so much that I decided to make witnessing one of my Love practices. Slowly but surely I began learning how to witness my own life and actions without judgment or criticism. That practice rippled out and began to transform how I witnessed the lives and actions of others. And as has happened with each of my practices, something radically shifted. Not only did my lifelong habit of self-loathing begin to dissipate, but I also began to see others through the eyes of Love. Witnessing transformed the way I move through the world by bringing me the kind of peace I never imagined to be possible.

Teflon or Velcro?

Have you ever seen one of those movies where a witness makes a deal with the government and gets sent off to live in a small town in the middle of nowhere as a "new person"?

Well, that's what the practice of witnessing does—without the moving van. We get to walk away from our old lives as fear's mobsters and henchmen, from a lifetime spent kneecapping ourselves with our old stories encasing our hearts in cement and throwing them into the river never to be seen again. We discover how to live in Love by learning to witness ourselves and others without judgment or criticism.

Although this practice is amazing, I would be lying to you if I didn't tell you that witnessing also has its challenges. Until you try it, you won't realize how judgmental and critical you are all the time of everyone and everything—most especially yourself. Studies have shown that almost 80 percent of what we think about is negative or counter-productive. Let me repeat that because it is a mind-blowing statistic: we spend 80 percent of our time thinking negative, unproductive thoughts!

To make matters worse, studies also have shown that our brains are wired for what's called a "negativity bias." Scientists call this the "Teflon/Velcro phenomenon." We Teflon the good and Velcro the bad. In other words, we actually forget the delightful experiences we've had and hold on to the horrible instead.

This is why our heart-centered Love practices are essential. We need them in order to reprogram our individual fear-based operating systems. Our practices bring us back to the hearts of our True Selves, transforming not only our own lives but also the lives of those around us. As we learn to witness our own thoughts without judgment and criticism, the people with whom we interact feel and experience this change in our thinking. Consciousness creates reality, and by seeing ourselves through the lens of Love, we begin to see everyone else as expressions of that same Love and they begin to see us that way too.

YOUR PRACTICE OF WITNESSING

Witnessing allows us to become neutral observers of our own lives. When we do this, we begin to peel back layers that we never even knew were there. We experience ourselves and others in more open-minded and open-hearted ways as we start sloughing off a lot of old voices and old stories.

Witnessing can be both the easiest and the most challenging of practices because it will evolve or devolve as you do. It requires maintenance to keep it fresh. It needs to become habitual but not rote. Steady but not stilted.

Here are some guidelines for your practice:

- Your only goal is to observe your thoughts without judgment or criticism. Do not judge or criticize your thoughts.
- Whatever you witness in your own thinking, try not to react.
- However shocked or ashamed your own thoughts may make you feel, don't judge or shame yourself.
- Don't try to change your own thinking.
- Don't try to "think better."
- Instead, pay attention to patterns in your thinking.

🐚 Notice when you're afraid, but don't feed the fear.

🐚 Learn how to reassure yourself instead of judging yourself.

Consciously choose to do this for twenty minutes a day, but specifically try to do it when you feel out of sorts.

When I began my own witnessing practice, frankly I was shocked at how often my thoughts were anxious or angry, judgmental or jumpy, fretful or fearful, testy or tearful. But instead of mentally beating myself up for not being calmer or nicer or more grounded, I simply took notice of the patterns of my thinking. Instead of wishing my thoughts were "better," I began to recognize when I was acting from a place of Love as opposed to when fear was running the show. Immediately, I could feel the difference this made. What Ram Dass said would happen, did. I felt more like my True Self, which he describes as "pure consciousness, joy, compassion, the One." The more joy I felt, the less tied I felt to old ideas of some separate "me."

Over time, witnessing has become the way I center myself. Even on the worst days now, I'm never as ruffled or anxious or upset as I used to be. I feel much less attached to my old habitual reactions and responses.

But I won't lie! To do this requires daily, deliberate, conscious, and committed practice. It's ridiculously easy to lose the thread and wind up down that old rabbit hole of fear and judgment without even knowing it. It happens to us all. We start out the day in gratitude, take a walk, practice joy, but the first e-mail we get that yanks our chains or the first person who cuts us off in traffic, boom! In comes the judgment and the anger, and pretty soon all that Love practice has flown right out the window.

When this happens, what do we do? We practice witnessing! Remember: don't judge. Just observe. Remind yourself: it is what it is. Don't beat yourself up for it. Don't beat anyone else up for it. Just witness. And then do it again.

This is the whole practice. It's a cycle. All of our practices are.

- 🫀 We let our hearts lead us, even if we struggle with what we're learning.
- 🫀 We show up to joy and gratitude.
- 🫀 We witness our thoughts without judgment.
- 🫀 And when we need to, we create new heart-centered practices that keep our passion and our purpose firmly rooted and grounded in the Field of Love.

When we begin to have more faith in our heart-centered practices than we do in our old habits of fear, we'll begin to feel that peace that passes all understanding. When this happens, we'll know, in the hearts of our True Selves, that we are truly living Love.

5

THE PRACTICE
OF DISCERNMENT

Flowers or Weeds

This practice is one of my favorites and not just because it's inspired by my beloved friend and spiritual mentor Dee.

Dee taught me the deep spiritual truths that eventually became the foundation of this practice of discernment. After Dee died suddenly, I found myself thinking about the many life lessons she had shared with me. About a month before her passing, I'd planted a field of wild grasses and wildflowers. The guy who helped turn over the earth and seed it said to me, "I've taken out all the weeds, but once you start watering, they're going to come back. You're going to have to keep up with them." I spent the whole spring and summer tending to that field. As I did, I kept thinking about something Dee had often said. She told me that spiritual practice is like gardening. We have to be dedicated to weeding our spiritual garden every single day; removing every thought that's based in fear, anger, darkness, or doubt; and replacing those thoughts with Love.

I was in my late twenties the first time she shared that metaphor with me, and I had no clue about practice. My first thought was *Can't I just hire a gardener from time to time? I mean, what's so bad about a few weeds?*

Dee saw it as her mission to never stop reminding me that we only have two choices—fear or Love—and that choosing Love requires commitment, consistency, and hard work. In other words, we have to weed. No one else can do it for us.

In the months following Dee's death, I had to weed like crazy. A whole patch of nightshade, which is poisonous, came up right in the middle of some California poppies, and I had to carefully pull out the weeds so that the flowers could grow. Another time, these things I thought were pretty little pink morning glories started sprouting up, and it wasn't until I saw they were taking over the whole meadow and choking out everything else that I realized I'd been suckered in by their beauty. I had to rip up five garbage bags of bindweed before it killed everything else.

Every day I weeded, I thought of Dee. Wherever she was, apparently she knew I still had this to learn: we have to weed every day. Weed when it is tiring, weed when it is boring, weed when we want to believe that a few weeds don't matter or that they seem as pretty as the flowers. Weed when weeding is the last thing we want to do.

That summer, I weeded not only my garden but also my thoughts. I weeded out every fear so that Love could grow. From time to time, I came across a perfect patch of meadow filled with wild grasses and flowers, and I'd picture my beloved friend in a beautiful garden somewhere, weeding away, grinning that mischievous grin she had. It was as if she knew that, finally, I was weeding too, both of us doing our work, understanding at last that this is what we are here to do: *weed out the fear and let Love bloom.*

After I began my witnessing practice, I saw that, despite my best efforts, I still got duped into old habits of thoughts. Although learning to neutrally observe my own thinking had centered my heart in Love, when I fell for fear, boy, did I fall down that old rabbit hole from which it felt almost impossible to climb out. What would help prevent that? I began thinking: what if I looked at my thoughts and, without judgment, tried to determine whether they were weeds or flowers? I tried it, and it worked! As I witnessed my thoughts, I weeded them. The more I did this, the more I found myself in the Field of Love surrounded by flowers!

Of course, there always will be days and weeks and months when we find ourselves back in the throes of old fears. After all, as my favorite aunt liked to say with a wry grin, "We haven't ascended yet!" That's precisely why I love this discernment practice. We either can look at the overgrown gardens of our lives and hate ourselves for letting them get so tangled and tattered or we can get back out there and start to weed again.

Weeding Your Garden

Write This Down

> I want to . . .
> or
> I would like to . . .
> or
> I wish I could . . .

Then pull out your notebook and do a ten-minute freewrite about any or all of these prompts. As always, allow whatever needs to surface to come up. Don't edit your words. Don't judge. Don't stop writing. Just let it all out.

Once you have finished freewriting—and then stood up, stretched, cleared your head—I want you to read through what you have written and see which ideas seem like flowers and which ones seem like weeds. Remember: flowers are the ideas that we plant and nurture and water and prune in order to help them grow and bloom. Or more simply put: flowers = Love.

Weeds are the ideas that will prevent our garden from growing. Weeds can choke out the flowers or use up all the nutrients in the soil or flat out take over the whole garden. In other words: weeds = fear.

When weeding, be especially vigilant about the weeds that may come up looking like flowers. These are thoughts or ideas that seem loving at first glance (*I want to be less angry* or *I want to keep believing that I deserve to find a loving partner*).

Like my flouncy pink flowers that ended up being totally destructive, certain thoughts initially may seem loving, but when you dig a little deeper, you find fear.

When you see a flower, write "FLOWER" next to it. But when you see a weed, I want you to imagine what it will take to pull that weed out of your garden. Does it have shallow roots or deep ones? Do you find yourself resisting getting rid of this weed? Witness what you are feeling and then remind yourself that you have to get that weed out. Picture yourself weeding, and as you do, cross out what you have written. Pull that thought out of your thought garden and toss it.

Then, when all the weeds have been removed, go back to each flower and draw a little picture of whatever flower that thought evokes: tulip, lilac, daisy, sunflower. Have fun with this! Pull out your colored pencils. Remember: this is a variation on witnessing, so don't judge your thoughts or your fun. But do weed your garden.

This freewriting helps fertilize the soil of your discernment practice.

YOUR PRACTICE OF DISCERNMENT

Once your freewriting gets your discernment practice flowing, you'll find there are lots of ways to weed your garden and practice discernment. As you develop your own practice, you can begin to find the ones that work best for you. In the meantime, here are a few to try. Once you get the hang of it, try making up your own.

Weed as You Go. If you find that you're falling into the habit of negative fearful thinking, commit to spending twenty minutes a day witnessing every thought you have and mentally calling them out: *Flower. Weed. Weed. Weed. Flower.* If it's a weed, picture yourself pulling it out of the loamy soil of your garden and chucking it aside. If it's a flower, take the time to visualize it and then enjoy and be grateful for it. This discernment between flowers and weeds, without judgment, is a powerful practice.

Weed in the Morning. Every morning, commit to making the first five to ten minutes of each day an opportunity to witness and to weed. No matter what comes to thought— whether it's a morning prayer or your to-do list, witness and weed. But always remember: smell the roses!

Weed at Night. Recap your day by witnessing your thoughts that arise. This isn't about judging something to be a weed and another thing a flower. This is about discerning what you think about what happened. This is important because what we carry with us from day to day determines how we experience our life. So as you witness what thoughts arise about something that happened, if you find yourself feeling judgmental or fearful or anxious, weed those feelings out. Don't let them linger in your garden. Then, when you have removed all the weeds, revisit the flower thoughts. And as you drift off to sleep, picture each one blooming in your beautiful garden that is the Field of Love.

Weed Out Your Problems. When you're trying to figure out what to do or how you feel about something, take out your journal and divide your page into two columns. On one side, write "Weeds." On the other, write "Flowers." Then begin to think about your problem. As thoughts arise, if they feel like weeds, write them down in the Weeds column. If they feel like flowers, put them down under Flowers. Weed thoughts are fear thoughts, angry thoughts, anxious thoughts, judgmental and critical thoughts. Flower thoughts are rooted in Love.

These are not pros and cons. In fact, you may find something you decided you had an excellent reason for doing is actually a choice made from a place of fear. What you are witnessing are the thoughts you have about a problem or issue in your life. When you've written down all the weeds and flowers, put a huge X through the weeds. Then go back and read through your flowers. These are your heart-centered choices. Let them be your guide in assessing how you want to address whatever problem or issue has come up to.

Weed the World. Every single day we're bombarded with fear after fear after fear, be it in the news or in social media. Instead of taking them in, try weeding what you hear and read. Is this Facebook post or that news report based in fear or grounded in Love? Choose what thoughts you want to have in your garden. Choose to live in the Field of Love.

There are countless ways to practice discernment. I hope that some of these will spark you to create your own practices!

These are your only criteria:

Judge not.

Only observe.

Choose Love, not fear.

Most important of all: keep practicing heart-centered discernment every single day.

6

THE PRACTICE
of AWARENESS

Stop *Shoulding* All over Yourself

As in our gardens, the hardest weeds to pull out in our lives are the ones with the deepest roots. Those are the ones that got planted a long time ago.

As the child of famous parents, I often asked myself, *How can I live up to the expectations everyone has of me based on my parents and my privileged upbringing?* How can I be true to myself by living as who I really am inside? I was struggling to figure out who I was supposed to be based on who I and everyone I knew thought I *should* be.

Now let's be real. These are first-world problems to have. I wasn't trying to figure out how to escape abuse or poverty. But that didn't mean I was immune to fear's siren call. And the more fear gained my ear, the less Love I heard.

To the younger me, both questions seemed equally valid. My parents loved me. I had an incredible life. Why wouldn't I want to live up to who my parents hoped I would become? Why shouldn't I pay forward the privilege into which I had been born by making a difference in the lives of others?

What I couldn't see then is, of course, patently clear now. I always got hung up in the same place, on one word that, when it crops up, points back to fear. Replacing that word in your vocabulary is your next step on your journey to becoming a Love practitioner.

The word *should* is the most insidious and noxious weed of all! *Should* can talk us into anything—convincing us to buy this product, take this magic pill or potion, be afraid of this idea, join this group—in order to buy into fear's latest safety scheme. *Should* separates us from other people, our minds from our hearts, us from our True Selves. Whether *should* makes us feel superior (he *should* have known better than to marry her) or inferior (I *should* have known better than to eat that quart of ice cream), it always makes us feel separated from Love. That is how fear gets our ear, and we start writing our stories in fear's ink. We begin to feel farther away from the Field of Love, and so we seek safety in a place or in someone or in an idea.

Here's the good news: no matter how much fear has *shoulded* all over our lives, Love will always be stronger than fear. All the fear-based stories we have come to believe are us are NOT! *Remove should; you find good.*

Write This Down

I should . . .

Then, once a day, freewrite to see what surfaces.

You can focus it on a particular topic or you can open it up to anything. There are only two rules:

- ❦ Don't edit yourself.
- ❦ Don't stop until you hear the voice of your True Self.

To illustrate what I mean by this, I'm going to share a short *should* journal entry of my own:

I should stop eating chocolate every day. It may be raw dark chocolate, but it's still chocolate—and I eat it every day. Even when I don't eat it, I want to eat it. Am I addicted to chocolate? Sure, there are worse addictions, but an addiction is an addiction. And speaking of addictions, I should also learn how to be less busy. This morning I wanted to meditate, but instead I updated my operating systems. On every single device. I should be better at meditation. I should make it more of a priority. I should walk my talk. I should be choosing Love. Or at least feel guilty when I do not choose Love. Or maybe that's all wrong. Maybe I shouldn't feel guilty about anything. I should feel less guilty and more present. I should . . . oh, this one is huge: I should be better about staying in touch with people. I'm terrible at that. I should answer e-mails and texts more consistently. That's just basic human kindness. Bottom line, I should be more loving.

NO! NO! STOP! ENOUGH! This isn't loving at all.

As I hope you can see, this exercise is about giving voice to the verbal vomit of *should* we don't realize we carry around every day. We *should* all over ourselves all the time. It's what we do with all our *shoulds* that makes all the difference. This exercise helps us begin to purge the *shoulding* that has infiltrated our lives and then come back home to our Field of Love, beyond all wrongdoing and right-doing.

Getting Underneath Your *Should*

Should freewriting often starts with something we truly believe we should do. Although I love chocolate and eat only "healthy" raw dark chocolate, not a day goes by when I don't question whether I'm addicted to it. So the *should* I started with felt real.

When our *shoulds* seems reasonable, we start to converse with them as if this were a totally normal thing to do. And then we're sunk. Because once we're arguing with our *shoulds,* we've fallen into the habit of fear. When I'm caught up worrying whether I *should* or should't be eating chocolate, then what I'm really saying is I'm worried I'm eating too much chocolate. I'm worried that I'm addicted. In other words, I'm just plain afraid. And whatever decision I make from a place of fear won't be a good one—guaranteed. The moment we let one *should* in the door, the other *shoulds* will start bubbling up until suddenly we're puking *shoulds* all over the page.

Funnily enough, that is actually the beauty of this practice. However unpleasant it may feel, purging is useful because it allows us to see how subtle and multifarious our *shoulds* are. Doing this will go a long way to starting to shift our habits of fear because, eventually, there will come a point where you feel—in the marrow of your being—how smarmy and slimy *shoulds* really are and how they've taken you miles away from anyone you ever wanted to be. When we feel this, the voice of our True Selves is finally being heard. That's when we get to stop writing and shout how *shoulding* all over ourselves makes us feel—as I did with that huge NO! NO! STOP! ENOUGH!

Then it's time to take a little breather. Get up, stretch, go outside. Because when you come back, it's time to call on some of the discernment you've been practicing.

YOUR PRACTICE OF AWARENESS

Shoulds are a whole lot of fears trying to make themselves heard. So, after our *shoulds* surface, the next thing we need to do is translate them. In other words, we have to figure out what fear is trying to get us to believe.

The decoder ring of all *shoulding* is really simple: *should = I'm afraid.*

When I wrote that I *should* stop eating chocolate every day, fear was trying to get me to believe that I'm out of control, that I'm an addict, and that I *should* be afraid of that part of myself. When I wrote that I *should* learn how to be less busy, fear was telling me that all the progress I've made in becoming less of a workaholic has been for naught. Fear was calling me a fraud. From there, fear kept going with the subterranean ticker tape of fears that run in the background of all our daily operating systems. This exercise is the antivirus that we need on a regular basis to clean everything up!

It wasn't until all the shame and guilt exploded all over the page that I came to my senses. My practices of witnessing, weeding, choosing Love, and reconnecting with my True Self came to the rescue like the superheroes that they are! Suddenly, I viscerally felt how wrong all this *shoulding* feels. "This is not you!" my True Self yelled.

Although I'm always stunned that there are still so many ways that fear tricks me into *shoulding* all over myself, the *shoulding* spell inevitably gets broken by the voice of Love.

Once we are listening to Love, we can move on to the last and most important part of this exercise: redirecting ourselves back to the Field of Love by replacing *should* with *good*. We do this by drilling down beneath the *should* to reframe it into good. Here's what I mean by that:

Chocolate

- ❧ I love chocolate, but I don't love it when it feels like a compulsion.
- ❧ I really would like to be more mindful about food in general.
- ❧ I am going to practice being more present and grateful as I eat.

Workaholism

- ❧ You are *not* the person you used to be. You have learned how to be kinder and more present and way less compulsive.
- ❧ Stop letting fear trick you into thinking you can regress to positions outgrown.

Meditation

- ❧ You may not be the best meditator, but look how far you have come!
- ❧ You do take the time to be quiet and to pray. You do have a contemplative practice. Many contemplative practices in fact.
- ❧ Don't let fear make you believe lies about yourself.
- ❧ Take this as a gentle reminder to prioritize meditation tomorrow morning. You know you feel better when you do.

This is how you, too, can learn to practice awareness and translate *should* into *good*. Here are some guidelines that will ease you into your own practice:

- ❧ Start out by speaking directly to fear's argument, but don't be fooled into arguing back.
- ❧ Agree to disagree with fear. Then begin to find the truth to fear's counterfeit.
- ❧ Discern the positive and hold to that.
- ❧ Look for the learning. Let your *shoulds* lead you toward what you may need to release or areas that need growth.

❧ Use these as potential seeds for new heart-centered Love practices.

❧ Release the *should* and hold only to the *good.*

Once we can begin to see fear's arguments as the con game they are, we'll be increasingly able to tune back into our True Selves speaking the language of Love. Then we find out what it is we really need to hear and move forward with hope and healing! We've turned *should* into *good* . . . into awareness and practice and promise. Instead of being bludgeoned by fear or fooled into fixing a problem, we are living Love.

Once you get the hang of it, this practice of awareness won't require lengthy freewriting. The more we see the *should*, the less we keep *shoulding* all over ourselves. Through this beautiful daily, deliberate, conscious, and committed practice, we are continually pulling up the weeds and leaving only the flowers—which, of course, is the only thing that ever grows in the Field of Love.

7

THE PRACTICE
OF FORGIVENESS

The Stories of Our Lives

This practice trifecta—witnessing, discernment, and awareness—lays the groundwork for the next part of our journey: identifying and releasing our core old stories. This is big, powerful, intense, and deeply transformative work.

When I was a twenty-year-old college student, I read this quote by the poet Adrienne Rich: "The stories of our lives become our lives." It seemed like an invitation and a warning. So I thought about it a lot as I was trying to figure out how to become an adult. I often asked myself, "What story do I want to write with my life?" This invited me to see my future as a blank page of hopeful possibility. But when that same blank page became filled with doubts and fears, it also felt like a warning: *What if these old stories about not being enough, of lack and loneliness and loss, are the stories that become my life?*

Rich's words have circled back to me throughout my life. Whenever I've battled with my own self-loathing, I've asked myself, "Which stories have led me to this anxious, workaholic, self-hating life I seem to be living?" Inevitably, as I practiced my way out of the darkness of fear and back into the light of Love, I discovered some stories that had become so engrained that I thought they were "me." Only by weeding my garden every day was I able to unearth the deeply buried roots of these core old stories that needed to be yanked out for good.

We all have these core old stories. From the moment we can think, we begin to write our lives. At first we write in the voice of our True Self. The language spoken by our True Selves is always the language of Love.

So when and why do we start tuning out Love and listening more to the fear-based voices of others? How do we end up crafting our lives using a template that bears less and less resemblance to the wildly original tale of our True Selves?

Our old stories weren't created in isolation. We learned to be storytellers because we ourselves absorbed the stories that were told to us. Stories which have come down through centuries. We all write the narratives of our lives with the ink of the past flowing through the pens of our imagined futures.

When we hear a story, we remember it because our hearts have in some way been engaged. Stories bring ideas to life by infusing them with color, depth, meaning, and emotion. Over time, human beings have become hardwired to learn through the telling of tales. When we see our lives as stories, we can share our hard-earned life lessons with others in ways that everyone can remember.

Stories are wonderful! It is just our attachment to them that becomes problematic, especially if we view them as gospel. So if we get stuck in our stories, we have to learn to get unstuck.

My first clue about how to unstick myself came from observing other people. I noticed that whenever I began a friendship, I shared my stories. And so did my new friends. This is how we humans get to know each other. Then I began to see an interesting phenomenon. There were always certain narratives that loomed large across my new friends' lives. It is as though they handed me a book called *This Is Me* and then highlighted all the important bits. As I result, I could see the way these accounts manifested in their daily actions, choices, and beliefs.

My mother left us when I was three. By the time I was five, I was standing on a chair to cook for my sisters and brothers. I never really had a childhood. I became an adult before I knew how to be one. Now that I'm retired, I often feel guilty for not working and taking care of just myself.

My father dropped dead when I was twelve. He was my champion, and without him, my whole life fell apart. Since he left, I've never felt like anyone else could ever understand me. That's probably why I've never been able to have a long-term relationship.

My mother beat me, and when she was done, she told me to pray to God to prove myself worthy of God's love. Whenever I start something new, I beat myself up with the same fear: I'm not worthy. I'll never be good enough.

My new friends told me these stories to explain who they are, why they do what they do, think what they think, love the way they love, fear what they fear. They were perfectly aware of how these stories have played out in their lives. They told them as a way of sharing their most intimate fears but also as a kind of disclaimer: this is why I am who I am. These were their core old stories.

Of course, I was doing the same thing. We all have core stories and most of us can't seem to shake them. We all carry around life-limiting narratives that shape everything we believe and every decision we make.

I decided it was time to stop accepting my core old stories as etched in stone, so I began to write about them. In particular, I wrote about three difficult conversations with my mother that happened when I was young. They had become my excuses for everything that had ever gone wrong. They were stories told by fear about fear, and they had been imprinted in me. They surfaced whenever something triggered them. If I felt fearful about money or doubtful that I had any skills or gifts or talents, my core old stores told me that I *should* be afraid, that I was not worthy of succeeding, and that there was no one who could or would ever help me. More than anything, these old stories made me believe that I didn't deserve the life I longed to lead. They ended up taking me further away from the Field of Love.

Before I decided to write them down, I'd often tried to stop listening to those tall tales. But until I was willing to completely let go of my core old stories, until I recognized that I would never be able to erase fear's stories using the mindset that had created them, nothing was going to change. To release myself, I had to learn how to stop conversing with fear.

Once upon a Time

I love hearing the poet David Whyte tell one of his favorite stories—about the Tuatha De Danna, a mystical Irish tribe "devoted to beauty and artistry." When their land was invaded, the Tuatha De Danna fought their foes. Twice they failed. So when the third battle came, they arrived in full colorful battle regalia. But as the marauders rushed toward them, instead of fighting, the Tuatha De Danna turned sideways into the light and disappeared.

Whyte goes on to say, "Sometimes we have to turn sideways into the light to our life-limiting narratives and archaic voices, to the conversations that have kept us in the darkness—and disappear to them."

This was what I had to learn how to do, and my heart-centered practices have taught me how. They can teach you how, as well. Through witnessing, discernment, and awareness, slowly but surely we can begin to see which fear-based stories of our lives have come to seem like our lives. Then, by reengaging with Love, we can disappear to them and let them go!

Once upon a time, we heard less of fear and more of Love. Once upon a time, the things we now believe bring us safety and security seemed like crazy made-up adult ideas. Once upon a time, we honored our True Selves and spoke the language of Love in fluency and joy. Once upon a time we laughed at fear and saw it for the illusion it is.

Once upon a time is now. It's time for us to write our stories once again using the language of Love.

My Dead Husband

Identifying your core stories is the first step in letting them go. This can begin to happen through the process of witnessing. Do you notice that there are certain narratives that you hear yourself telling over and over again, that you always recount whenever you meet someone new?

When I met my best friend, Pamela, I quickly noticed there was one story she told repeatedly. To be sure, it was powerful. It also was what had led her to the work she was doing. So there were many "good" and "legitimate" reasons for her to share that story. But something about the way she told it kept niggling me. Finally, I said something.

"Do you know that every time you meet someone new, within the first five minutes you tell people about your dead husband?"

She looked at me with an expression of surprise and not a little annoyance. "Well, it's the reason I'm doing what I'm doing. I started this nonprofit because of what happened when he was sick. I am sharing his story as a way of connecting with people who had similar experiences to my own."

I told her I recognized that, but it also felt to me like she was sharing his story as a way of justifying her own existence. I asked whether this rang true.

She agreed to think about it, and we didn't talk much about it for a while. But the reason Pamela and I are best friends is because we've always been each other's spiritual workout partners. Eventually, she began to share things that helped us both see that what I had intuited had merit. Her relationship to her husband and his illness had, indeed, inspired her to create her nonprofit, which helped give people suffering through illness and other major issues a voice. But her relationship to him, his illness, and the abusive addictive behavior that had resurfaced when he was sick, had also almost killed her.

Finally, she had to make a choice. She could stay with him until he died, if she didn't die too. Or she could choose to save her own life, even though it meant walking away from someone who was dying, whom she still loved deeply. The guilt she felt about making the latter choice was so overwhelming that she never told anyone what had happened. Instead, she kept bringing "her dead husband" into every new encounter in her life.

As she began to forgive herself and him, she gradually released that core old story of guilt and fear and shame. As she did, she freed not only herself but also her husband. Now he lives in her heart in the place of pure Love, which had been the truth of their connection. This is living Love.

These days, whenever Pamela and I are counseling someone who is carrying around a core story weighing them down with guilt and fear and shame, we humorously refer to it as their "dead husband story." It's a reminder to us that we always have to keep removing the albatrosses from around our necks, which keep us tied to fear and forgetting to listen to Love.

Rewriting Our Old Stories

Our next exercise will help you identify and release *your* core old stories. You're going to learn how to be detectives on the hunt for clues to your own life. The clues you're looking for are the reasons that certain stories stick when countless others don't. Unfortunately, however, you won't find the answer in how you've been telling them. You're going to have to look deeper!

Most of us have been telling our old stories for so long that we're absolutely sure they happened that way. This is never true! No matter how fixed and firm and foundational one may seem, it is only a story. And stories are always fiction.

No matter how vivid a memory may be, no one can ever really know exactly what happened in the past, including you. Because the moment something happens, we start processing it. And when we do, what actually happened begins to shift and change from a real event into a story. Furthermore, what happens for one person is never the same for another person. Two people can be in the same place at the same time, experiencing the same thing, and what one remembers may be radically different from what another person does.

The only events that become lasting memories are what the brilliant memoirist Patricia Hampl calls "images of value." In other words, we remember what we cherish. But which "we" is doing the cherishing? This is the first question you need to ask yourself as you journal your core old stories. Here's one clue: if you remember something that feels hurtful or painful or challenging, it's probably not your True Self that's doing the remembering. Because the only thing that our True Self ever sees, feels, or cherishes is Love.

This exercise involves writing and rewriting and rewriting some more, because only by writing "beneath" the familiar narratives will you begin to discover why these core old stories have stuck like gum to the soul of your existence.

As I began writing my own core old stories, I was able to recognize they were all moments during which my mother had shared "important life lessons" with me. Although she intended well, each of these lessons ended up making me feel that I didn't deserve something: money, creativity, success, support. And whaddaya know? Those have been the big areas of struggle for me my whole life. Why? The more I wrote, the more I realized that these three incidents had stuck in my memory because what my mom said had made me feel *afraid*. *Afraid* that I didn't deserve money, would never be truly creative, would have to struggle to succeed, and that no one in my family would ever support me. I Velcroed these stories, and they kept me in fear.

Although there were countless instances of my parents showing me love and support, encouraging and paying for my creativity, the fear engendered in me during those early childhood moments stuck! Writing and then rewriting my core stories allowed me to begin to unearth what I believed to be true and what I had not yet allowed myself to know.

Now it's your turn!

Write This Down

The story I tell the most . . .
This is the conversation I keep having in my head . . .
My "dead husband story" is . . .
This is "who I am" . . .

Using one or all of these freewriting prompts, start the process of seeing what surfaces when you write for ten minutes without picking up your pen from the page.

Here are some ideas for ways to focus your freewriting:

- 🐦 Write your story as though you were sharing it with a new friend.
- 🐦 Remember little details: smells or tastes or sounds or colors.
- 🐦 Record why you think you have remembered this story.
- 🐦 Write about the people in this story.

Once you feel that you have identified a core old story, freewrite about it every day to dive in more deeply.

Here are some ways to approach this:

- ৶ Write about your confusion. Why does this keep coming up? Why does it still affect me? Why does it even still matter?
- ৶ Jot down any hunches you may have. Nothing is too ridiculous or far-fetched. You will be amazed at what fear can get us to believe.
- ৶ Note any questions that surface. Try freewriting all questions and no answers.
- ৶ Write the story as you always tell it. Then rewrite it as your True Self.
- ৶ Record all the ways this story keeps surfacing.

As you do all this, you'll begin to see what it is you have been cherishing, why you have held on to something, what you are still trying to understand or process. The more you do this, the less hold it will have on you. But if something still feels sticky, try more freewriting. Ask yourself:

- ৶ What am I having trouble releasing? Or who am I having trouble releasing?
- ৶ What am I feeling about this story? Where in my body is it?
- ৶ Is there someone in this story who brings up these feelings? Is there somebody in my life right now who is a trigger?

Eventually, through your freewriting, you will come smack up against the core of your core old story. You'll know it when you feel it. This is the response mechanism triggered whenever your old story is triggered. You not only will feel it, but you'll also be able to witness its effects: your most reliable practices fall by the wayside. Your rational mind goes out the window. You act without thinking, you feel without feeling good, you react without control.

When this happens, go back to your witnessing practice. Keep at it until you can witness this trigger mechanism without reacting to it. Don't judge yourself, but keep observing the response and what provokes it. Your witnessing will win the day, and you will be less at the mercy of these triggers.

As this triggering response begins to ease, you'll realize that there is something, someone, some thought, or some perception of yourself that you need to release.

Amazing Grace

A few years ago, I heard this story and it cracked open my heart:

Following the dissolution of apartheid in South Africa, a commission was formed to try to make reparations for the atrocities that had been inflicted on the black communities. Trials were held, overseen by a group called the Truth and Reconciliation Commission. It was at one of these trials that an elderly black woman came face to face with an Afrikaans man who had killed her son in front of her and then had come back to kidnap her husband, eventually forcing her to watch the man she loved be burned to death. As her husband's body was being doused with gasoline, he prayed, "Father, forgive them."

Now this woman was being given the opportunity to right the wrongs that had been done to her. She was asked how justice could be served to the man who had destroyed her family.

She stood up and said, "I want three things."

First, she asked to be taken back to the place where her husband's body had been burned so that she could gather up the dust and give him a proper burial.

Then she said, "My husband and son were my only family. I want secondly, therefore, for this man to become my son. I would like for him to come twice a month to the ghetto and spend a day with me so that I can pour out on him whatever love I still have remaining in me.

"And, finally, I want a third thing. This was also the wish of my husband. I would kindly ask someone to lead me across the courtroom so that I can take this man in my arms and embrace him and let him know that he is truly forgiven."

This powerful story gave me the model for my practice of forgiveness. Because once I had journaled about my core old stories for a few months, it became clear that the only way I was going to release them was to learn how to forgive. And the person I needed to forgive was my mother.

I was able to see that although my mom might well have made different choices in how she shared her life lessons with me, she said what she said and did what she did because she thought she was being loving. In truth, however, she'd been guided by fear. And I had simply Velcroed her fear!

When I understood that, my whole perspective changed. I felt a huge wave of compassion for my fearful mom. Suddenly, instead of seeing her as a less-than-perfect parent, I saw her through the eyes of unconditional Love, which is to say I saw her the way I had always hoped she would see me. To see through the eyes of Love is forgiveness. To see others as we wish to be seen: with, in, as, and through Love. To love others as we wish we were loved.

This living Love is the essence of your next heart-centered practice: the conscious practice of forgiveness.

Most of us already have a long-established relationship to forgiveness. From the time I was little I was able to see that the reason people did "bad things" was because they were afraid—even the people who seemed to hurt me. I knew they would have done better had they been able to. I could recognize that their fear was running the show. So I knew that to forgive them wasn't about letting them off the hook or saying they hadn't been hurtful. Rather I understood that, if I held them in Love, Love would do the healing.

My greater difficulty was forgiving myself for never ever being as good or as kind or as honest or as hardworking or as evolved—or as anything—as I hoped to be. Never. Ever. Enough. I could never forgive myself for that, and I could certainly never see why anyone else would forgive me either. I was too stuck in fear to let Love in.

Fear is like the water that finally breaks a dam and floods everything in its path. Water has been pushing up against every area of that dam for ages, but the place where it gets through is where the dam is weakest. For some of us, our weakest spots are where an inflated sense of self runs riot. Fear urges us to promote, preserve, and protect our ego kingdoms against people or ideas that might take them away from us.

For others, our weakest points are the things we hate about ourselves. Fear shuts us down by telling us how terrible we are, how we'll never amount to anything, how all we do is fail and hurt others through our failures.

For most of us, it's a little of both. But either way, it's only fear. And answering fear with fear just keeps us in fear. We have to invite Love in to do the talking. That's where forgiveness comes in. The language of forgiveness, as that story of the woman in South Africa showed, is always and only Love.

Dr. Martin Luther King Jr. expressed this so beautifully: "Darkness cannot drive out darkness; only light can do that. Hate cannot drive out hate; only Love can do that." When we forgive, how we remember things changes too. Then we can use the lessons of the past to build a future on Love.

YOUR PRACTICE OF FORGIVENESS

As you begin to explore your own practice of forgiveness in releasing your core old stories, consider these essential qualities to bring you into alignment with the essence of

Victoria Price

the amazing grace expressed by that extraordinary South African woman:

- 💗 Forgiveness doesn't mean we forget. It means we remember through a different lens.
- 💗 Forgiveness doesn't mean we condone. It means we understand the cause of others' actions, and we choose to act differently.
- 💗 Forgiveness doesn't mean we shut down our emotions. It means we invite Love to shift out of fear into healing.

To practice forgiveness is to practice Love.

We forgive by:

- 💗 loving every day;
- 💗 loving even when we feel that we should be allowed to hate;
- 💗 loving when we feel resentment;
- 💗 loving when we're angry; and
- 💗 inviting anyone and everyone who seems to have hurt us back into our hearts and embracing them in Love.

How do we do this? We don't! Love does. All we have to do is to invite Love into our hearts every single day and then let Love move through us.

Perhaps this sounds ridiculous to you—a little like renovating a decrepit tenement by covering it in pink paint. That's certainly what fear would have you believe. But if you learn anything from reading this book, I hope it's this: *we* are not doing the healing; Love is. Through our heart-centered practices, we are consciously inviting Love back into our lives. When we do, it is Love that erases fear through forgiveness. In other words, we forgive ourselves and others by inviting Love back into our hearts. We don't forget or condone or deny our own or anyone else's past actions. We simply recognize and acknowledge that fear was running the show, but now we've vowed to keep living Love.

This is the game changer. This is the conscious practice of forgiveness.

8

THE PRACTICE
OF CENTERING

There Is No Me, Only We

I hope that as you're working through the heart-centered Love practices in this book, you're beginning to experience a return to your True Self like a quiet homecoming. I love how James Finley describes this: "In utter simplicity, we intuitively realize within ourselves that our existence, though truly our own, is as the waves to the sea, as the light is to the flame." When we come home to our True Selves by living Love, we start to remember that we've never left the Field of Love. Suddenly, all the energy we've put into showing up to our own lives and fixing what ails us is replaced by the deep assurance that we never ever actually left home at all.

As this homecoming manifests itself in our lives, glorious things happen. Some of these may seem strange to the people in our lives who aren't accompanying us on this journey. This happened to me.

When I began to reconnect with my True Self, I no longer needed or wanted to celebrate my birthday, though I was happy to celebrate other people's birthdays. This idea didn't go over well with those closest to me, who wanted to lovingly acknowledge "my special day." I was told that my no-birthday idea was selfish, disingenuous, and impractical. So sometimes it was easier to do the birthday thing than to get into the nitty-gritty of why this actually mattered to me. But as my Love practice began to transform my life, I finally worked up the courage to tell the truth about the reason for my request. After that, it stopped being a problem. Now I get a few happy birthday texts, but that's about it. What changed? Well, frankly, I think my reason sounded so flat-out weird that it's become easier for everyone to avoid the topic altogether.

Maybe it won't sound any less weird to you than it did to my loved ones: I don't celebrate my birthday because I don't believe that our births are our beginnings any more than I believe that our deaths are our endings. I wanted to stop celebrating an illusion. Instead, I longed to spend a quiet day of spiritual reflection and reconnection in the truth of the Field of Love, holding to what has become the single most soothing thing in my entire spiritual arsenal—an idea that too often slips out of consciousness during the hustle and bustle of everyday life:

This me I have spent my whole life trying to become is not
the real me.
There is no me.
There is only we.

A few years ago, on an airplane somewhere over the North Atlantic, I was praying to feel a sense of release from all the pressures of my life. As I stared out the window into the starry night sky, I heard these words: *There is no me. There is only we.* The next thing I knew, I actually felt this persona I'd spent my whole life becoming float up from my body and fly out the window into the galaxy. I drifted off into a sweet and dreamless sleep, and when I woke up to the sun rising pink and gold over Europe, I felt a calm freedom and pure joy that I'd never known before.

Since then, I can honestly say the greatest gift of my spiritual practice has been the increasing realization that all we're really here to do is to heal that illusory lie of a separate I by living in Love. By practicing Love, we reconnect to our True Selves, to each other, to our world, and to the Universe of Spirit.

So if your eyes are't rolled too far back into your head and if you're willing to take this leap of faith with me, together we're going to dive into ways that you, too, can learn to unsee the lie of your own "I." You may hate this. You may love it. You may think this is flat-out nuts. You may decide this is the best thing since chocolate. All I ask is that you keep an open mind and an open heart. And if it seems wacky to you, try reading this like *Harry Potter* or *The Lord of the Rings*. It may sound like pure fantasy, but keep trying to go with the flow of Love.

No Self. No Problem.

Crazy as all this may sound, this isn't actually some half-baked notion I made up. Not only is this idea reflected in every spiritual and mythic tradition over thousands of years, but it's also affirmed by many cutting-edge contemporary scientific studies. Furthermore, almost everyone who has had a near death experience (NDE) has undergone something similar to what I felt when my old self flew out that airplane window. As neurosurgeon Dr. Eben Alexander described his own NDE:

> What I saw and learned there has placed me quite literally in a new world: a world where we are much more than our brains and bodies, and where death is not the end of consciousness but rather a chapter in a vast, and incalculably positive, journey. For most of my journey, someone else was with me. A woman. Without using any words, she spoke to me. The message went through me like a wind, and I instantly understood that it was true: "You are loved and cherished, dearly, forever. You have nothing to fear. There is nothing you can do wrong."

Aren't these the unconditionally loving words we've spent our whole lives longing to hear? We can, and we will—the more we're willing to give up our old ideas of who we thought we're supposed to be. The more we let go, the more unconditionally loved we will feel.

This release of self into unconditional Love is at the core of almost all spiritual teachings. On the night the Buddha reached enlightenment, what he saw clearly was that we do not exist as separate beings. He understood that we've simply become attached to our limited ideas of existence. Buddhist texts repeatedly describe the ways in which conscious-ness creates the world as a dream or mirage. Neuroscientist and consciousness researcher Dr. Anil Seth says the same thing: "The experience of being a person is so familiar, so unified, and so continuous that it is difficult not to take it for granted . . . we shouldn't take it for granted."

One of my favorite Buddhist writers, Jack Kornfield, tells us that our belief that we exist as individual selves is the "root illusion" that "causes suffering and removes us from the freedom and mystery of life [by] attaching to certain forms, feelings, desires, images, and actions." We stop suffering the more we release attachment.

Perhaps the greatest contribution of Eastern religions such as Buddhism and Hinduism to global thought has been to show us that there are only two causes of all human discontent: suffering and craving. They are flip sides of the same coin. It's never something or someone outside ourselves that disturbs us. When we believe that something, someone, some situation, some potential outcome, some fear, is making us miserable, it's our fixation on it that causes our suffering. Conversely, when we crave something, someone, some situation, some hoped-for outcome and then attribute our ongoing well-being to it or fear that it will come to an end, we end up back in suffering. It's an infinity loop of inner human misery. And at the root of that loop is our attachment to the fixed self. So why not let it go? Well, not if fear has anything to do with it!

Fear is a master magician using the classic ploy all magicians use to get us to believe every sleight of hand. It's called "misdirection." Magicians use misdirection to fool us into looking where they want us to look so that we won't see how we're being tricked. They do this by making us—their willing and eager audience—believe we're in control of our own thinking. We believe we're choosing to see what we want to see. Instead, we're seeing exactly what the magician is telling us to look at.

The illusion of a fixed self is fear's most brilliant misdirection! Fear wants us to believe that we're the source of our safety and that to lose that sense of self would be to lose control. We see what fear wants us to see.

Except that it's all an illusion!! Fear is an illusion. Our constructed sense of self is an illusion.

So what's the solution? To practice doing precisely what fear never wants us to do—losing control. When we do, as Jack Kornfield writes, "We find liberation and a spacious joy. Discovering emptiness brings a lightness of heart, flexibility, and an ease that rests in all things. The more solidly we grasp our identity, the more solid our problems become. Once I asked a delightful old Sri Lankan meditation master to teach me the essence of Buddhism. He just laughed and said three times, 'No self, no problem.'"

No self. No problem. That is the end of all suffering. So how do we get there? This next practice is one way.

YOUR PRACTICE OF CENTERING AND SURRENDER

No self. No problem. This may be the simplest practice, yet sometimes it can feel incredibly hard.

Here's the simple part: there's no writing, no thinking, no soul searching.

All you have to do is surrender yourself to the idea of no self.

How? By sitting or lying down, closing your eyes, and inviting Love in.

That's it.

Choose a quiet place where you can sit or lie down without distractions or interruptions for five to twenty minutes. Even the timing is up to you.

Get comfortable, and then close your eyes and begin to listen to your own breathing. As you start to hear the rhythm of your breath, begin to feel it in your body. Your lungs fill up and release, fill up and release.

Once you fall into this rhythm, with each breath, breathe in Love.

You may choose to do this by using the actual word. Breathe in and speak the word *Love* silently or out loud. You also may just feel or visualize it.

Experiment. There's no right way to do this practice, only your way.

After you've breathed in Love, then breathe out fear.

Again, you can speak fear, visualize fear, feel fear— whatever works for you. However you can release fear, go for it! If you want to expel fear a little more forcefully out of your lungs, do it! This is your practice.

Invite Love in with each incoming breath and then expel fear with each outgoing breath.

Breathe in: Love.

Breathe out: fear.

After a minute or so, your mind may begin to wander and you may not even realize it. Other thoughts will begin to drift in, and you'll go with them.

What kinds of thoughts? Every kind of thought!

I forgot to pick up the dry cleaning.

I want some ice cream.

What can I binge-watch tonight?

I wonder whether sloths are called "sloths" because people thought they were lazy or whether the word sloth actually came from the animal?

My back has been killing me for months now. What if something is really wrong?

Why can't my partner ever wash the dishes? It's always me cleaning up.

That golden retriever puppy I just saw sure was cute!

When a thought surfaces, don't judge it or yourself. But also don't engage with it. Instead, go back to your breathing.

Breathe in Love. Breathe out fear.

Even if a thought takes you down a long and winding road and, suddenly, you realize you can't remember how long you've been thinking about ice cream or sloths or puppies, just go back to your breathing and focus on breathing in Love and breathing out fear.

 Breathe in Love. Breathe out fear.

Even if the thought contains the cure for world hunger, the meaning of God, the location of the lost city of Atlantis, let it go!

I'm serious. No matter what the thought is, including the answer to all your own and the world's problems: Let. It. Go.

Breathe in Love. Breathe out fear.

Picture your thoughts as leaves upon a river and let them float by. And if you realize that you've picked up that thought, place it back in the river and go back to your breathing.

Breathe in Love. Breathe out fear.

You can set a timer or you can leave it open-ended. If you drift off to sleep, that's fine. You only have one task: Breathe in Love. Breathe out fear.

The challenging part is not that thoughts arise. They're going to arise. The challenging part isn't beating yourself up for being distracted by your thoughts and losing the thread of Love for a few seconds or even for long stretches of time. Because this will happen. Your thoughts absolutely will come in and try to take you out of Love. So a big part of what you need to practice is not beating yourself up for this. (This, too, is the practice of Love.) Instead, simply and gently and kindly turn back to your breath.

Breathe in Love. Breathe out fear.

This is the whole practice. It's a meditation or contemplative practice that can recalibrate our lifelong habits of any and every kind of thinking.

Like all Love practices, this metamorphosis can feel magical. When we commit to surrendering to something as simple as breathing in Love, we radically surrender our egos. Then Love begins to fill the places where fear-based thinking once reigned supreme. From there, everything changes. Inviting Love in and asking it to usher fear out begins to recalibrate our operating systems and wipe clean our hard drives. Where once we felt programmed by fear, we begin to remember that our only true language is Love.

When I can't sleep and my mind is racing in fear, I breathe in Love and breathe out fear. When I'm sitting in an airport surrounded by other anxious travelers, I close my eyes and breathe in Love and breathe out fear. When I wake up in the morning and my thoughts are lapping themselves on the racetrack of my to-do list, I stop and breathe in Love and breathe out fear. I remember in the core of my being that I've never stopped being rooted and grounded in Love, and I invite you to do the same.

No self. No problem.

Over time, I've created different iterations of this breathing practice, depending on what has come to me and through me. I always start by breathing in Love and breathing out fear. But sometimes, as I feel the fear clear, I want to breathe in Love and breathe that same Love back out into the world. So I do. I feel the Love that is centering me flow out and touch everything around me and encircle us all.

Breathe in Love. Breathe out Love.

When I feel particularly shaky and uncentered, I often use two words: *All Love.* As I breathe in, I consciously invite and surrender to the Infinite Allness of Love. Doing this is powerful if you are distracted or anxious in ways that seem especially persistent or scary.

Breathe in all. Breathe out Love.

You may find there are other variations that work for you. Sitting or lying down may feel the most soothing. You may want to set a timer. You may use this to fall asleep. This is *your* practice. You and Love are cocreating it.

These are your only guidelines:

- ॐ Be willing to surrender your habitual thoughts.
- ॐ Release judgment and attachment by consciously and continually returning your focus to Love.
- ॐ Focus on Love instead of the ticker tape of fear.

Love in. Love out. No self. No problem.

9

THE PRACTICE
OF UNKNOWING

Mystics in Our Midst

No self, no problem is not just a Buddhist idea. Many of the Christian mystics, such as Julian of Norwich, John of the Cross, Meister Eckhart, and the anonymous author of *The Cloud of Unknowing*, have written similar things about what happens when we practice letting go of our identities and egos. In fact, it was Mirabai Starr's gorgeous translation of John of the Cross that helped me in the creation of a practice I absolutely adore.

> *I entered into unknowing*
> *and remained there,*
> *knowing nothing.*
>
> *This place transcends all thought.*

Whoever arrives
in the land of unknowing
frees herself of herself.
Everything she thought she knew
falls away
and her consciousness expands
to enfold the whole universe.

This has been so true for me. I used to be the person you wanted on your Trivial Pursuit team. At one point I knew the birthdays of every player on the 1978 Los Angeles Dodgers and all the winners of the Academy Award for Best Picture. Now I can hardly remember where I took my walk yesterday. Instead what I do remember is the beautiful tree I saw or the way the sun warmed me when it came out from behind the clouds.

Sometimes, I'll admit, I do freak out a little when I realize how far away I am from the person I once was. *Where is that crackerjack mind of yours?* Fear whispers in my ear. (Fear likes to scare me with the idea that I have lost something I may never get back.) Then I remember how anxious that crackerjack mind used to feel and how lovely it now is, as John of the Cross wrote, to "rest in unknowing."

Feeling the relief that came from resting in unknowing when my life was going well, however, wasn't the only thing that inspired this next practice. It also took being thrown off a cliff into the complete unknown. That, and meeting a charming Welshman named Ilt, who travels the world scouting locations for movies.

Wherever Ilt goes, he plays this game with himself, one inspired by the writer and adventurer T. E. Lawrence (yes, that Lawrence . . . of Arabia). While hiking through the massive monolithic rockscapes of Wadi Rum in Jordan, Ilt found he couldn't get Lawrence's classic description of that epic desert landscape out of his mind: *vast, echoing, and godlike.* How fantastic, he thought, to be able to distill a place down to its essence. So now, wherever Ilt goes, he finds three perfect words for each place.

Later that night, on my drive home, I found I couldn't stop thinking about Ilt's three words. As my windshield wipers pounded out a steady rhythm against an unexpected late spring snow, three of my own words matched the metronymic movement of the blades. The same three words, over and over again, that had been playing through my mind all week.

However, they didn't describe some incredible geographic place in the world but rather *my* place in the world. And those three words sure didn't make my heart sing like Lawrence's words had for Ilt. In fact, my three words felt pretty darn uncomfortable, a little bit shameful, embarrassing even. They formed a phrase that I had been taught my whole life to resist, to avoid, to fear.

I don't know.

That was the year my life fell apart, and I chose not to reassemble it. Instead, I embraced the unknown.

One night while I was working out of town, I made the mistake of looking at my e-mails when I couldn't sleep at two in the morning. That taught me one of the greatest lessons of my life: never read your e-mails at 2:00 a.m.!

Seriously. Don't do it! If you get good news, you'll be so excited that you won't be able to go back to sleep. And no one else wants to be woken up at 2:00 a.m. to hear your good news. And if you get bad news, it will always seem way worse in the middle of the night. All you'll do is get more anxious about it. So if you take nothing else away from reading this book, remember: *nothing good can come of reading your e-mails at 2:00 a.m.*

In *my* 2:00 a.m. e-mail, I found out that I had nine weeks to vacate the house where I'd been living, because my landlord needed to sell it. Nine weeks! And I was going to be home for only three of them. To make matters worse, I had jury duty!

Although I worked on the road about 250 days a year, I absolutely adored where I lived. The thought of giving up my home filled me with panic. So the first thing I did was to try to find a temporary place to live. But nothing fell into place. No matter what I tried, no solution arose.

I knew why. From the moment I found out I had to leave my home, I had heard the reason come through loud and clear, as though someone were whispering in my ear. I just didn't want to listen. Yet each time my next quick fix fell through, the same words came through again and again and again: *"Let it all go."*

There was only one problem: I didn't want to let it all go.

As the weeks dwindled, I realized I had no choice. Finally, I made up my mind to do what was being asked of me: let go of my life as it had been and create a new practice of "intentional homelessness." I would commit to living on the road for at least two years without a home of my own. Not only that, but I wouldn't plan what would happen after those two years. I only would commit to waking up each morning and being present to wherever I was, to whatever was happening, and to whatever needed to happen. I would stop seeking safety in a specific place or job description. I would step on to the high dive and jump into the joy of my life!

That was the spring I met Ilt and realized that my three words were *I don't know*. Since then I have faced the fears I thought I never would have had the chutzpah to stare down. I found the kind of faith I only had dreamed of having. And I found a freedom beyond my wildest imaginings.

Sound crazy? It's not actually! But I didn't know that then. All I knew was that I didn't know anything about what lay ahead—and that felt helpless and hopeful at the same time. But I did know one thing: I had a choice. I could keep letting *I don't know* scare me, or I could make friends with it and allow it to lead me. Guess which one I chose?

Invoking Your "I Don't Know"

This practice will help you take three words that scare the heck out of almost every person on the planet and befriend them. This is the deliberate practice of invoking your *I don't know*.

To invoke means . . .

a) to call on something for inspiration;

b) to appeal to something (or someone) as an authority.

Basically, this practice is about choosing to be inspired by what we cannot know about our lives instead of letting it scare us. It's also about learning to let what we don't know be our guide.

Why on earth would anyone want to do this? Because this is how we lean on the source that ultimately does our truest knowing for us. This source, of course, is Love.

However, this is not what fear would have us believe. Fear wants us to think that the remedy for anything which scares us is safety and control. But safe and controlled isn't how it actually ends up playing out. The more fear we let into our thinking, the less secure we feel. Because the more fearful we are, the less we experience the presence of Love. The only way to let go of fear is to risk facing precisely what fear has told us never to do: face the ultimate fear, the fear of the unknown.

Psychologists call the fear of the unknown "The One Fear to Rule Them All." It is the fundamental fear underlying all fears.

What happens when we die?
How would we handle losing everything?
How will we face a grave illness or the death of a loved one?
What if we haven't saved enough for retirement?
What if we get fired?

At the beginning, middle, and end of those questions lies our terror of what we don't know. But we weren't always scared by not knowing. As kids, we *knew* we didn't know much. But instead of that causing fear, it was the source of our curiosity, our joy, our thirst for adventure. As children, we invoked "I don't know" constantly. We also lived much more in the Field of Love. That is not a coincidence.

It wasn't until we got older and began to crave more safety and control that we began to fear more and Love less. Over time that became our new norm, and therefore more and more invisible to us. That's why it often takes everything falling apart for us to be willing to risk losing control. Because let's face it: when we start to lose control, we feel out of control.

Here is what I have learned:

What we don't know will usually scare us.
What we don't know will ultimately set us free.

When we're faced with a big question in our lives, we all have the same impulse: find an answer. Sometimes it feels like any answer will do. Anything to feel like we have things back under control. That's what we've been taught.

As students, we were rewarded for finding the right answers. That same pattern has followed us through our whole lives, conditioning us to believe that an answer always will make things better. So when we have a problem, some of us call our go-to people for advice. Some of us pray. Others try to listen to their guts or make a list of pros and cons. Eventually, however, we choose an answer that will assuage our discomfort with what we don't know.

But how often do we go through this whole process only to end up wondering whether we've come up with the "right answer" after all? This is because most of us don't know what we really feel!

We went to school and learned about history and the periodic table and how to take a standardized test. All that really demonstrated was whether we were good at finding answers. But did anyone ever ask us how we *felt* about anything? Did anyone let us know that how our hearts feel about something is actually way more important than facts or SATs?

We grow up totally unprepared to be human. And so we start to seek safety in the identities and institutions that everyone else tells us will make us feel safe. Until one day we realize that all that supposed safety hasn't made us feel any more safe or confident or happy or free. Finally, from that place of not knowing what to do next to change our lives, we are willing to invoke our *"I don't knows."*

Write This Down

I don't know . . .

Then pull out your journal, find a clean page, clear out ten minutes of your life, and start writing without stopping. You can do this as an everyday practice, or you can do it the next time you feel scared or unsure or flat-out terrified of a big looming "I don't know."

Freewriting your "I don't know" keeps you from running toward an imaginary "right answer." Instead, you're inviting your "I don't know" in.

Admit to yourself:

- ℰ *I don't know* what to do.
- ℰ *I don't know* what I feel.
- ℰ *I don't know* what to think.
- ℰ *I don't know* what's going to happen.
- ℰ Own your *I don't know.*
- ℰ Befriend your *I don't know.*
- ℰ Learn to love your *I don't know.*

Because guess what? You *don't* know. Admitting and accepting this feels true, and the truth always feels like a relief. But don't worry if, after that initial *phew!*, what surfaces are your fears of what you don't know. Fear is no fan of the truth, and so the moment you accept your *I don't know,* fear will usually try to have a field day with you.

Just keep writing. Let it all out. Every single fear—from the ones that seem absolutely true to the most sky-is-falling ridiculous ones. Get them out of your head and on to the paper. Often writing or speaking our fears will go a long way toward releasing them. But if, as you get to the end of your freewriting, you find yourself still feeling the fear of what you don't know, don't be alarmed. That is what the next part of this practice is all about. It's time to face your fears. And you already have the tools!

YOUR PRACTICE OF UNKNOWING

If giving voice to what you don't know has left you feeling afraid, it's time to call on what you've learned from your other Love practices:

- ☙ Witness the fear. Don't judge it. Simply notice it neutrally and do a little weeding.
- ☙ Try talking with patience and kindness to the part of you that's freaked out.
- ☙ Remind yourself: of course, this is scary. I was never taught how to trust my gut or listen to my heart.

Sometimes when I'm being barraged by fear, it helps me to laugh. Fear is ridiculously unoriginal, always trotting out the same damn argument over and over again. "Seriously," I say to fear, "this again? The world is not flat, and I am not going to sail over the edge of the earth."

Other times, when laughter feels impossible because I'm quaking in my boots, I try to speak to myself as I wish some parent or teacher had.

"Hey, sweetheart, of course this is scary. Of course it isn't comfortable not knowing what's going to happen. But think about it. Your whole life you haven't known what would happen when you got on that plane or started that relationship or bought that business. Sometimes it was amazing. Sometimes not so much. But you're stronger than ever. So take a deep breath and trust that Love has got your back like always. You're going to be okay."

Doing this helps me diffuse the intensity of the fear.

Once we disempower the grip of fear even a little, we open the door for Love. Love is always there. It's just that we can't always feel it. Release even a little fear and suddenly you can feel the Love that heals.

So the first part of invoking "I don't know" is facing your fears with compassion, kindness, and trust. Because each time we're willing to face down the fears that flood us, we begin to dismantle them. Slowly, but surely, we find ourselves leaving that limiting loop of behavior that threatened to keep us stuck forever. When we do, we begin to feel the faith we've developed in the healing power of Love.

Find Your Own Faith

Faith is a tricky word for some of us. But it's an important part of all heart-centered Love practices.

Recently, I was able to ask Father Richard Rohr how he talks about faith to people who are terrified that they have none, are not religious, don't believe in any kind of higher power, or have lost the faith they once had. He paused for a minute and then said, "At the end of the day, *faith* is just another word for *trust.*"

To trust is to believe. We all believe in something—in the love of our family and friends, in the sun rising, in nature, in animals, or in the power of good. But deep down I believe what we believe in most of all is the power of Love.

Faith in Love is no Hallmark card. Faith in Love is radical and redemptive. It takes guts to believe in something that also can sound like fairy dust and unicorns. That's why creating heart-centered practices is important. We might not be able to explain what Love is, but when we feel its effects, we sure as heck recognize its powerful presence. Faith in

Love is what makes us willing to stop relying on the "stinkin' thinkin'" that has built up all the ways we thought we would feel safe in the world. Faith in Love allows us to release our old ways of knowing and let Love do the knowing for us.

When you witness the fears that arise and find the courage to invoke your "I don't know," you will feel an empty unknowable space. This kind of space may have made you anxious in the past. It's probably the kind of space you've wanted to fill with answers. My go-to behavior to assuage the anxiety of what I didn't know was always to work harder; think more; do more; try anything to outrun, outsmart, outmaneuver, outpace my fear of the unknown. It never worked because it just postponed the inevitable. Our fears will always catch up with us, especially if we're meeting fear with fear. But I didn't get that. So when fear told me that I didn't have enough money to pay the bills, that someone was angry with me, that some fresh hell was going to break loose, I threw everything I had at fear in the form of hard work, new ideas, brainstorming, and getting busy. Doing something—anything—instead of feeling the fear.

Until one day . . . and another day . . . and another day, all that doing stopped working. And fear was sitting in the passenger seat next to me, with no intention of getting out of the car.

Feeling my faith began rather simply: I reminded myself that I've always been okay. It was nothing highfalutin or fancy. In fact, it had to be simple for me to believe it. I remembered how, even when I was afraid of what I didn't have, I always had enough. When I was afraid I was unlovable, someone always loved me. When I was afraid I was a terrible person, someone always reflected back my goodness.

I began to feel all the ways that Love has manifested in my life. I started to see that everything exciting and transformative and amazing that has happened in my life began with "I don't know." What I didn't know always ended up taking me exactly where I needed to go!

I began to think of *I don't know* as an invitation to Love. By consciously invoking *I don't know* every time I had a question I couldn't answer or one that brought anxiety or doubt or fear, something profound began to shift. I acknowledged that my daily human life always would be riddled with *I don't knows*. And then I consciously chose to turn all of my *I don't knows* over to Love.

So if you're struggling with faith, remember:

🐘 You don't have to know. Love knows all.

🐘 Trust that you've never left the Field of Love.

🐘 Trust your practice of living Love. Your practices are your parachutes, and you will always land in Love.

Free Your Self

Remember that person I told you about who looked in the mirror and vowed to change her life? That person who tried to keep that vow over and over again? First, she discovered the power of practicing joy and gratitude. Then she began witnessing and weeding out her *shoulds*. Finally, she embraced her *I don't know*. Now, that person who tried so hard to do everything right and had ended up miserable? She's gone.

I may not know what's around the bend or how the next problem will be solved, but I have faith that Love does. I'm not nearly as afraid anymore because I feel a kind of freedom I never could have imagined possible.

That is what my deliberate practice of *I don't know* has done for me, and it's exactly what yours can do for you. It will help you face your fears instead of finding a false assurance that there is a "right answer." It will help you rediscover your faith in the power of Love. And it will bring you the freedom you always have craved.

Now, you just have to commit to showing up to everything that you don't know—which will come up more often once you start this practice— in a daily, deliberate, conscious, and committed way.

How you show up is, of course, up to you. There is no right way. *Heart-centered Love practices are always improvisational, never prescriptive.* What brings me joy may not bring you joy. The way I witness myself without judgment may not ring true for you at all. What you don't know is what you don't know, so no one can tell you how not to know it. But here are some guidelines:

🐚 Evolve your own practice of *I don't know* so that you can learn to hear your True Self talking in the language of Love, which you've been longing to hear your whole life.

❦ Invoke your *I don't know* where you once looked for outside answers.

❦ Face your fears instead of letting them loom into huge scary monsters.

❦ Find your faith in all the ways Love always has been there for you.

Finally, be willing over and over again to free yourself from the lies of fear and keep living Love.

10

THE PRACTICE
OF ACCEPTANCE

Dear Me!

When I was younger, I felt like I was just dying to make a difference, to hate myself less, to do anything to change the things that I despised about my life! Little did I know that I would have to die to be alive.

In my spiritual study, one of the most common threads I've discovered across centuries and traditions is the necessity of experiencing little deaths in order to open our hearts and minds to the higher power of Love. These little deaths are our willing—or more often unwilling—release of thoughts, habits, beliefs, ideas, or ideologies we've cherished as the source of our safety and security, as the manifestations of life and love—even of that which we hold most sacred. *We have to be willing to die to fear in order to live in Love.*

At first, this scared me . . . as the word *death* does for so many of us.

Then I read something that Father Richard Rohr wrote: "All the world can give us is small thinking, a small mind. But small mind, without the unitive experience of big mind, makes us feel unbearably alone. We feel lost, existentially guilty, and often fragile and powerless. A lot of guilt is . . . often a guilt about not having yet lived. . . . There is a certain fear of death that comes from not having lived yet. . . . There is an existential terror about losing what you have never found. Something in us says, 'I haven't done *it* yet.' I haven't experienced the stream of life yet. I haven't touched the real, the good, the true, and the beautiful—which is, of course, what we were created for. . . . If we have never lived, we will be terrified of death."

I was raised by three immensely successful and talented parents in a town where being "someone" meant everything because the whole world looked to Hollywood for ideas of what being "someone" meant. So I grew up feeling that the only thing that really mattered in life was figuring out who I was supposed to be and making a showy success of it. I was terrified that I wouldn't become "someone" before I died. As a teenager, I feared dying young. As I grew older, I feared living a long life and dying before I had truly lived.

You would think that would have been enough motivation for me to be that "someone." But of course something always held me back. It was neither opportunity nor talent nor desire. Nor was it my old stories and psychic stumbling blocks. What held me back was fear. I was dying to feel alive, yet scared to die never having lived.

Looking back now at the caged hamster that was me, spinning around on the same wheel of fear day after month after year after decade, I know now that all I had to do was step off into Love and live. But to do that, something had to die. Actually, many somethings: the little lies I believed about what life is supposed to be. I had to wake up to what life really is: Love.

This came through to me so beautifully on a recent trip, which helped me remember all I've learned over the course of my life's journey.

When I was in my early thirties, I moved to Paris.

My father had died six months earlier. After taking care of him during the last two-and-a-half years of his life and then settling his estate, I did what I always did in those days when I didn't know how to soothe my anxiety. I got busy being busy, making big plans and putting them into action in order to keep the hard things I didn't want to feel at bay.

I had always wanted to move back to Europe, where I'd lived as a teenager. It was there that I believed the creative iconoclastic existence I had long imagined for myself would finally materialize.

Instead, in that beautiful City of Light, my life proceeded to dismantle itself.

I had gone to Paris with a partner and big dreams for our life together. When I returned to the United States later that year, it was with my tail between my legs, alone and utterly clueless about who I was and what I was supposed to be or do or think or feel about anything and everything.

While living in Paris, day after day I struggled to find a way to survive the deepest sorrow and anxiety and loneliness I had ever known. It was only because I was starting to develop a spiritual practice that I never gave in to those demons. But neither did I truly face them, which is why, I know now, they kept resurfacing in countless ways.

Ultimately, these practices have not only saved my life, but also have brought me that dreamed-of creative iconoclastic existence filled with grace and growth, joy and connection, and so much Love.

When I recently found myself back in Paris for work, I had a revelation. As I checked into my Airbnb that was, uncannily, on the same street on which I had lived, I realized that it was exactly twenty-five years to the date when I had moved there. For the next nine days, I did many of the things I had done a quarter-century earlier: shopped at the same grocery stores, visited the same museums, ate the same food at the same restaurants, and even went to the French Open with the same dear friend. I was being given a chance to revisit a living movie of my old self and take stock of who I had been.

On my last afternoon, in the rain, I decided to walk back to my lodgings. As I tramped aimlessly through puddles and down tiny alleys, peeked into eclectic shops and hidden gardens, I was flooded with memories of discovering all these places for the first time. Except that back then, wandering those streets did not feel joyful and connected and hopeful and true. It had felt like I was trying to outrun my own anxiety and loneliness, yet never succeeding.

Meandering my soggy way home on that cold and wet late spring day, I remembered how isolated and afraid I used to feel while walking those same streets all those years ago. How I worried about what people thought of the way I looked or acted or spoke. I remembered the fear I felt about what my life would hold and the terror of not knowing if I ever would figure out who I was supposed to be.

I was strolling right beside that younger me on that rainy afternoon. I could feel her tension, her anxiety, her isolation. I remembered how she dreaded going home to the sweet apartment she had rented and how unnerved she felt by her loneliness. I recalled how she had tried to reassure herself. Although the first stirrings of my spiritual practice had begun to soothe me, what I really thought made me feel safe was that I felt financially secure, attractive, and safe in deep friendships with people whom I trusted would always be around.

I began talking to the younger me. "If I had told you then that all those things you thought would be your saving graces (your comfortable bank account, your youthful good looks, your deep friendships) would be taken away from you— not once, but over and over again—you would have been so terrified, wouldn't you? You thought those things would make everything okay. But, actually, it was all the letting go that has saved you, all the loss that has been your gain. The money, the people, the youth, the reputation—those never mattered. The spiritual practice you were starting back then—that did. You've lost fortunes and careers and relationships and beauty. If you had known that then, you never would have been able to imagine that you would be walking these streets now with a kind of joy that you didn't even know existed, would you?"

It was true! Now I was walking through cold wet dreary Paris, hunched under an umbrella with my hoodie pulled up against the dampness, yet filled with an inner joy and light and connectedness and confidence and hope that the younger me (with her money and her friendships and her future and her youth) had never ever felt. How could I have imagined that losing what I thought was important would gift me the life I had always longed for?

The gift of hindsight is the insight it offers us for the choices we're making right now. When we can see how the things we thought we needed are not what we actually do need, how the things we feared the most rarely come to pass, how the greatest disappointments teach us the most, we can use those lessons to give us the courage to make the hard choices right now. That is the beauty of this next practice. It allows us to be our own guides and mentors in making new choices about how we move through our lives.

YOUR PRACTICE OF ACCEPTANCE

This is the most intimate of our heart-centered practices. You're going to practice Love by writing love letters to yourself. I hope this doesn't sound as silly as it might have when you first became a Love practitioner. But if it does, if you feel some blowback, remember that's fear talking and you don't have to listen!

As with so many of these practices, there can be many variations to fit your needs. By now, I hope you feel the freedom to know that you can cocreate this (and any) practice for yourself. So I'm going to suggest a few approaches that have meant a lot to me, and you can take it from there. Read these first and then try to make writing Love letters to yourself part of your regular heart-centered Love practice routine.

Write This Down

Dear Younger Me,

Then take out your journal, clear out ten minutes of time, and without editing or censoring, write a letter to your younger self.

Here are some suggestions that may help you identify your younger self:

- ❧ This can be you at any age, from childhood to a few years ago.
- ❧ You can choose a particular moment that you remember when you felt most fully yourself or when you felt hurt.
- ❧ This might be you at the time of one of your core old stories.
- ❧ It can be a you that was forgotten and whom you want to reclaim.

🌀 It can be a you whom you are ashamed of and want to forgive.

Here are some guidelines to focus your freewriting:

🌀 Write as the Love practitioner you've become. Write in the voice of your True Self. Write as Love, through Love, in Love, to Love.

🌀 Never judge yourself, even if you're writing to a younger self that you're not particularly proud of.

🌀 Write without knowing the ending. You may have started this letter to your younger self with an idea of what you wanted to "accomplish." Let that go. Let this freewriting take you where you need to go.

Inspired by my Parisian walk, I began playing with freewriting as a way of connecting with my younger self in areas of my life where I still felt stuck in my old stories, where I had resentments or regrets, and where I needed to find forgiveness for others or myself. It not only allowed me to let go of the stickiness in my past, but it also shifted my perspective on who I had been and who I am now and then accept all those versions of me. This brought me to a new variation on this practice, which I think you will enjoy.

Write This Down

Dear Future Me,

In this freewriting, you're going to write a letter to yourself sometime in the future. Here are some general suggestions and guidelines:

🐘 It can be a specific time in the future. This is useful if you're focused on a particular event, such as the birth of a child, a promotion, retirement.

🐘 This can be used as a way of addressing something you're afraid of, such as illness or money issues. By writing to your imagined self, you can witness the strength that comes from leaning on Love.

🐘 Again, write as the Love practitioner you've become. Write in the voice of your True Self—as Love, through Love, in Love, to Love. And write without knowing or outlining the ending.

This practice reminds us that the greatest gift we can give ourselves and each other is to lean on Love and let Love do our talking. It also serves to remind us of the strength of Love. Fear would have us believe that it is the tough guy and that Love is some ephemeral pipe dream filled with carnations and floating hearts. Wrong! Love, as I hope you are seeing, is the only power. Knowing this in our innermost hearts is why this final iteration on this practice may be the most important.

Tough Love

Most of us have a rocky relationship with the term "tough love." It can conjure up unpleasant memories of the adults in our past who did things to us that didn't feel loving, because they "loved" us or because it was "good" for us. My mother taught me important things such as discipline and self-reliance in ways that created both scars and blessings. And yet when I look back on what she instilled, I see that she was the one who gave me most of the spiritual survival tools that have gotten me to where I am now. In the long run, I feel grateful for my mother's tough love, although that wasn't always the case. In fact, it wasn't until I began working with a spiritual practitioner when I was in my thirties that I really fell in love with tough Love.

I could tell my practitioner anything, and she always heard it through Love. I felt Love loving me through her. This is why, when she sometimes got firm with me, calling me out if I was down a rabbit hole, I could listen without being defensive or hurt. I knew this was Love using my practitioner's voice to wake me up!

Over the years, I began to understand that Love sometimes needs to do whatever it takes to get us to listen. If we're in the throes of fear, sometimes tough Love doesn't feel good. This is because shifting out of fear and back into Love is like moving out of a comfort zone. Tough Love feels tough to fear! That's why we have to learn how to stop taking fear's side if we want to live in the Field of Love.

This tough Love freewriting practice has really helped me in the thorniest areas of my life, such as my often rocky relationship with food. When all I can think about is when and what and where will I get to eat next! I hate how this feels! I'm not listening to my True Self but instead I'm assuaging my anxiety or stress with food. Tough Love breaks this cycle by inviting Love in to do what Love does: Love us back whole, with total acceptance.

Write This Down

Dear Me! I know you feel . . .

Freewrite a letter from your True Self, rooted and grounded in Love, to the you who is struggling with something in particular or a general malaise. Whatever you're feeling, this letter is an opportunity for you to address the problem by turning to Love. You're going to write yourself what you want to hear from Love. Because, as I hope you're learning from our practices, Love is not "out there" someplace. Love is inside us. As you're writing with, through, and as the voice of Love, let Love guide you where you need to go.

Here are a few guidelines to focus this practice:

- 🐚 Write to your struggling self in the language of tough Love, the Love that knows the answers you can't seem to hear right now.
- 🐚 Don't judge or criticize yourself.
- 🐚 Listen for what Love wants you to hear.
- 🐚 Trust that Love knows the way, even when you feel you don't.
- 🐚 Lean into Love for your answers, even if fear doesn't like those answers.
- 🐚 Do not reply to fear. Keep speaking as your True Self to your True Self in the language of Love.

- ♡ Don't avoid saying the hard things, but always say them in Love.
- ♡ Remember that Love is strong, so you are strong. Love is all-powerful, so you are all-powerful. This is tough Love!

As you do your freewriting, understand that what you are really practicing is accepting your True Self, And remember: your True Self knows the truth: we can never ever live outside the Field of Love!

11

THE PRACTICE
OF PRESENCE

From Nobody to Everybody

"We all came into this world gifted with innocence, but gradually, as we became more intelligent, we lost our innocence. We were born with silence, and as we grew up, we lost the silence and were filled with words. We lived in our hearts, and as time passed, we moved into our heads. Now the reversal of this journey is enlightenment. It is the journey from head back to the heart, from words back to silence; getting back to our innocence in spite of our intelligence. Although very simple, this is a great achievement. Knowledge should lead you to that beautiful point of "I don't know." . . . Our whole evolution . . . is from being somebody to being nobody and from being nobody to being everybody."

—Sri Sri Ravi Shankar

N ow that I've become a dedicated Love practitioner, I'll be honest: sometimes I feel as though I'm "losing my mind." Not as in going crazy though, but as in literally losing all the ways I thought I was supposed to think about everything.

What a relief!

I used to believe that my mind was my safety net. Now I understand that the small mind that planned and schemed and thought everything through was not *my* mind at all. It was the mind of fear.

When we begin to practice Love, we begin to wake up from the stupor of fear. When we begin to wake up, fear panics, because it feels like it's being displaced. But that's actually not what's happening. Fear is not being displaced; it is being erased. The malware of fear is removed as our hard drives are wiped clean by Love.

So of course it can feel disconcerting to witness the erasure of everything we've spent our whole lives trying to be. As this starts to happen, we feel both less *and* more. Less tied to our stories and safety nets, less comfortable as we start to relinquish our old habits, while simultaneously more aware that we are stepping into uncharted territory, which paradoxically makes us feel more present and joyful and true.

Fear will always feel its erasure as a kind of death because fear, in fact, *is* dying. This is a good thing, though fear wouldn't want you to believe that. For as our fear-based learned sense-of-self begins to dissipate, what's revealed is what has always been the only true foundation of existence: the bedrock of Love.

As we let go of the idea that our fear-based brains are our safety nets, our intuitive Love-based understanding increasingly feels true. We access this heart-centered understanding through the great panacea of practice, because practice shows us how to die to our small selves so that we can live in Love.

When we begin to let who we thought we should be die off, we run up against something that feels both incredibly liberating and utterly terrifying. Bereft of all our old ideas of who we were, we feel the presence of the vast empty space of possibility. This is what we have wanted our whole lives, but now that it's before us, we don't know how to fill it! That's because we're not meant to fill it. We're simply meant to be present to exactly what is! But that's a hard lesson to learn, because after a lifetime of filling up all the cracks and crevices of our existence with busyness, most of us are not good at just being.

The reason problem-solving always felt so natural to us is because it allowed us to keep our fear-based mind-sets intact. That kept us comfortable in our familiar discomfort. Now that we're choosing to live Love, our old scripts sometimes don't match our new lives. But, tempting though it may be, the answer isn't just to write new scripts. The answer is to practice presence.

There's a reason that Eckhart Tolle's *The Power of Now* is one of the best-selling spiritual books of the past half-century. It's because he has articulated one of the most obvious yet least recognized truths of human existence: "Nothing has happened in the past; it happened in the now. Nothing will ever happen in the future; it will happen in the now." The only moment that we are ever truly "in" is this moment. Right now.

We forget that. We spend our lives either caught up in past memories or regrets and planning for or worrying about our futures. It's time to stop that cycle by learning how to be present right now. Through our heart-centered Love practices, we learn how to stop unconsciously carrying forward all of our old stories even as we step into being who we have always longed to become. This is presence. Tolle wrote, "The past perpetuates itself through lack of presence. The quality of your consciousness at this moment is what shapes the future." In other words, by not being present right here, right now, we let our old stories dictate not only our immediate actions but also the course of our future lives. This is why it's important to have our present consciousness be Love consciousness.

As we've been learning, however, if we start out looking at what hasn't worked in the past and then try to fix it (as in "I wasn't very present in the past and I want to be more present in the future"), we are sunk before we get out of the harbor. Why? Because that's not presence! That is past and future, but it's definitely not now! So in order to practice presence, we have to practice presence. We need to be present right here, right now. When we do that, we go from being somebody to being nobody and then from being nobody to being everybody. Because to be present is to finally feel—with every fiber of our beings—that we are all one in Love.

Pay Attention. Be Astonished. Tell about It.

A few years ago, I was on one of my daily practice of joy morning walks in a beautiful hilly neighborhood I love in Austin, Texas. The sun was shining, birds were singing, and flowers were blooming. I smiled as I chatted with people I met and petted their dogs. It was a glorious day.

Then I happened to look down at my phone, where I saw an e-mail that led me to another e-mail, which led me to my calendar, which led me to Google something, which led me smack into the back of a large SUV! I wasn't hurt, but I was mortified. And not just because someone actually saw me do it and tsked at me. I was embarrassed because one of the most essential parts of my daily practice of joy is being present right where I am . . . and clearly that hadn't gone very well!

I realized I had to up my game. If it was this easy to not be present while practicing presence, I asked myself, "How often am I not present during the rest of the day?" It was time to create a heart-centered practice of presence!

To do that, I turned to one of my great gurus—Mary Oliver. Oliver spent her life immersed in the natural world, which brought her joy and meaning and purpose. She shared her experiences with the rest of us through her poetry.

From the moment I read this poem, it became my mantra:

Instructions for living a life.
Pay attention.
Be astonished.
Tell about it.

Oliver's words guided me out of my fear of sharing my spiritual journey into becoming a joy practitioner and blogger by reminding me how extraordinary life is and encouraging me to share its wonders with others. It seemed the perfect inspiration for a new practice of presence.

Then I stumbled upon another poem by Oliver and decided to combine both into this wonder-full heart-centered practice. In this poem, she asks eight questions:

What did you notice?
What did you hear?
When did you admire?
What astonished you?
What would you like to see again?
What was most tender?
What was most wonderful?
What did you think was happening?

At the beginning of the day, at the beginning of a walk, at the beginning of a meeting or any kind of encounter, I remind myself: *Pay attention. Be astonished. Tell about it.* Then, during a walk, if I see something that catches my attention or have a conversation with another walker, I ask myself one of the eight questions: *What did you notice? What did you hear? When did you admire? What astonished you? What would you like to see again? What was most tender? What was most wonderful? What did you think was happening?* I take my time to answer. Then, once a day or after a particular experience, I sit down and freewrite and respond to all eight questions.

This practice proved so powerful because it gave me permission to look more deeply, to hear more carefully, to invest more of my heart, and to seek meaning where perhaps I had assumed meaning might not exist. Mostly, it invited me to be present more fully.

YOUR PRACTICE OF PRESENCE

This, too, is your practice. As you move out into the world, remind yourself to:

- 🐌 pay attention;
- 🐌 be astonished;
- 🐌 tell about it.

Then start asking yourself Oliver's eight questions and see where they take you.

So much of what we do requires very little attention. We drive large vehicles very fast in the company of other large vehicles going very fast, using very little of our consciousness. We brush our teeth, walk up and down stairs, feed ourselves, and drift off to sleep only vaguely aware of what we're doing. We are not paying attention! So when we do, we begin to see so much of what we have missed and we're astonished.

As little kids, we gave voice to this astonishment all the time. But as we grew up, we learned to silence our sense of wonder. What a mistake! When we remember the wonder in our lives, we feel connected in, as, and through Love—to our own hearts, to each other, and to our whole planet.

The beauty of this practice is that we are once again allowed to look in wonder at our own lives and share that wonder with others. This practice encourages us to shift out of our old routines and, instead, explore uncharted territory. The more you start paying attention, the more eager you become to really see things. This breaks us out of the ruts we all fall into and reminds us that to be afraid of exploring cheats us out of wonderful experiences. But even more important, this practice teaches us to be right here, right now—not in the past or the future, not in the old stories or the imagined ones. Even our same old same old stuff becomes more luminous as we shift out of our rote and fear-based thinking into looking through the lens of Love.

Presence is freedom. When we allow ourselves to be right where we are, we recognize that right here, right now is where we always have longed to be but never thought we would reach: in the presence of Love.

So, my Love practitioner companions, pay attention, be astonished, and please, tell me all about it!

12

THE PRACTICE OF OPENNESS

Love 24–7/365

Now that you're Love practitioners, what happens next? Well, it is still pretty much just like that old saying: Practice, practice, practice. Forever and ever. Amen. But now that you're feeling the Love, practice won't seem tedious or goal-oriented. At some point, practicing Love will even start to feel second nature. This is because it will feel just like what it is—like living Love.

This is what happens when we live Love. Instead of seeking joy, we practice joy. When we practice joy, we experience joy. Instead of trying to be more present, we practice presence. When we practice presence, we are more present. In whatever ways we practice Love, we feel more Love in our lives—guaranteed.

But I wouldn't be doing you any favors if I didn't prepare you for the inevitable ups and downs of practice. There will be days when you feel like you just don't want to practice. Days when your practice feels less like Love and more like duty. Days when joy or gratitude or surrender feel flat or perfunctory. Days when you flat out blow off Love. Which can lead to more days that you blow off Love. Which can turn into long stretches where you feel like you're doing everything but living Love.

Well, here's the good news: this, too, is all part of practice. In fact, it's why we practice in the first place. Because if we were all living Love 24–7/365 already, we wouldn't need practice. By continuing to practice what we seek, we begin to remember we've never stopped living in Love. No matter how lackluster our practice may sometimes feel, no matter how many times we blow it off, when we practice Love, we feel Love. Which reminds us that there is really nothing but Love.

Frankly, the more you practice, the less you'll need books like *Living Love*. But for now, we not only need practice, we also need each other. We need communities of Love practitioners to mirror Love and help us stay in our hearts and out of our heads, to keep turning a deaf ear to fear and to keep practicing—together.

We need to remind each other that Love always can erase the fears that try to bombard us. Fear is always going to keep trying to sell us its bill of goods. If the old way doesn't work, fear will try a new approach. It will get both more subtle and more outrageous. It will show up with new fears. It will speak its fears through the mouths of others, be it family, friends, or the media. It will convince us that there is something that cannot be transformed by Love.

We need to remind each other not to fight fear with fear, not to engage with fear, and certainly not to fear fear. We need to remind ourselves to keep practicing the Love that will always bring us back home to the hearts of our True Selves.

Practicing Love will always ask you to let go: to let go of explaining why practice works to the people in your life who think you're nuts. To let go of your old stories. To let go of needing approval or showing signs of progress that others can understand. If we're trying to prove to other people that what we're doing is working, it means that we're still giving fear our ear. Compare and despair, fear says. Instead, when we only listen to the language of Love, we don't need to prove anything to anyone. We are already unconditionally loved.

Nonetheless, sometimes it's hard to turn a deaf ear to the "loving worries" of well-intentioned family and friends. Remembering this is a huge help. It sounds loving when people who love us worry about our well-being, but more often it is fear.

As someone who has chosen to live "intentionally homeless" without the safety nets the world has told us we should have, I sometimes get anxious when I think about all the *shoulds* that I'm not obeying! Numbers in savings accounts. Concrete plans for the future. Four walls and a roof. When I think that way, I get pulled away from practicing what is actually working. I feel as though I've been yanked out of the arms of Love and am floundering around trying to finagle fear. That's when I have to just practice.

I don't have to find the "right practice." I only have to practice living Love. When I do, I always uncover the evidence I need, even if the evidence doesn't make sense to someone who isn't a Love practitioner. The evidence may be that I feel grateful for something that someone else sees as disastrous. The evidence might be a willingness to let go of something I've been holding on to for decades. The evidence might be that though I seem to have less, I am constantly receiving more. The evidence inevitably is that fear can't get my ear as easily and that I'm remembering to keep living Love.

This is why one of the most vital things that we can do as Love practitioners is to keep growing our practices. Keep them fresh instead of stale. Remember: fear is a big fan of the familiar. So if your practices start to feel less present or less conscious, it's always handy to have an ace in the hole like this next practice. It's one I learned from my dad, who taught me the meaning of joy and who showed me what Love feels like.

Practice Your Yes. Honor Your No.

A few years ago, I found a handwritten copy of the speech my father gave at my high school graduation. As I read it, I was flooded with sweet memories. I could hear my dad's voice on that long ago afternoon in June, as he read the short e. e. cummings poem that came at the end:

i thank you god
for most this amazing day

I remembered thinking to myself, *God?* My dad rarely talked about God in public. I wondered why he chose this particular poem.

for the leaping greenly spirit of trees
and a blue true dream of sky

Again, I was perplexed. Although he loved nature, truth be told, my dad would rather have spent a day with a painting of a tree than with a tree itself.

for everything which is infinite
which is natural

I'll be honest. By this time, my mind was beginning to wander. Like all Southern California high school graduates, our class would be spending the entire night at Disneyland and I couldn't wait!

Then he got to the last two lines:

which is
YES

That was when I knew why he had chosen the poem. It was that YES. Seeing it on the paper—written larger than all the rest—confirmed everything I've always known about my dad: *Yes* was his life philosophy. *Yes* was his prayer. *Yes* was his modus operandi. *Yes* was his spiritual practice. Every day my dad was grateful to his divine source for his life and the world around him. And every day he expressed his gratitude back to life in that word: *Yes*.

When I became an anxious, self-loathing workaholic, I lost my yes. By practicing Love, I rediscovered it. The more I lived my life guided by my yes, the more joy I felt, the more Love I shared, the more peace came into my life, the more fun I had, the more healing ensued. I had thought of myself as someone who had been saying yes to life but, actually, over time, the easy yes of my childhood had gotten whittled away by *should*, the doubts and fears and my to-do list. I had a partner who once told me that my nickname should have been Yeah But. Eventually Yeah But became Maybe and often just devolved into No.

Now, to be sure, there are times where having our no may be the most important thing in the world: creating boundaries, speaking our truths, taking care of ourselves instead of others. We all must learn to have our no. But saying yes to life is equally vital. It opens our hearts and minds. By saying yes, we're consenting to receive the Love that is always being given. Saying yes to Love expands our lives into connection with each other and with our planet.

YOUR PRACTICE OF OPENNESS

If you're ready, then say yes and dive right in!

> 🐢 The next time someone asks you to do something that doesn't seem like a risk to your well-being, say yes.

౿ Is there something your partner, spouse, or best friend has been asking you to do that you've had a million good reasons not to do? Say yes.

౿ Is there something you've always wanted to do or try? Say yes.

౿ Is there something that your True Self has been trying to get you to hear for a long time? Say yes and listen.

It's that simple.

It's a lifetime of letting fear run the show that makes saying yes seem so ridiculously hard. When I'm invited to do something that will keep me up later than my bedtime, my first instinct is always to say no. My reasons seem sound enough: I've been up too long already. I'm an early riser. I have a busy day coming up. What if I get tired? What if I don't get enough sleep and ruin my day tomorrow? Those excuses sound legit, but they're really just fear talking. Fear of what? That's the crazy part: there really is nothing to be afraid of. Granted, sometimes I do need to take care of myself and hit the hay early. But most of the time all my excuses are just fear wanting to be in control. And that's what I have to remember. Because I know that when I do say yes, I'll have an experience I never would have had otherwise. Be it wonderful or weird, interesting or illuminating, freaky or funny. And, most important, I will have chosen to live Love instead of staying rooted in fear.

As I've shared this practice with others, they all have experienced the same results on small and large scales.

They've told me how saying yes has radically opened their lives to changes they never thought they'd be able to make, things they never thought they'd have the courage to try: like weight loss, new careers, improv classes, traveling overseas, riding roller coasters, going out on a date. A musician from London shared with me that saying yes made her realize how much she always had said no. "People think of me as having a big personality and being so confident. But it took saying yes—and practicing saying yes—to realize how much of my life I've said no. Saying yes is helping me become the person that I've always wanted to be. Suddenly things are opening up for me, especially in my music. I'm getting gigs and really having the confidence to take them. It's amazing!"

To say yes instead of no (or maybe or yeah but) is to choose Love over fear. When we do this, our lives expand instead of contract. Saying yes actually reprograms our lives. Everything we do, every choice we make, creates the habits of thought and action with which we move through the world. We are our own computer programmers, and we write our own code every single minute of every single day. Like computers, we operate on a binary code. But our codes are not ones and zeroes. Our binary code comes down to yes and no, to Love and fear.

Saying no (having boundaries, respecting ourselves, recognizing when fear is a necessary warning system, acknowledging the red flags) is a necessary part of our binary code. But the other part is equally important: the yes to our hearts, the yes to each other, the yes to showing up and paying attention, the yes to our joy, the yes to our practice, the yes to living in Love.

When we're in our fear (our no), it's impossible to remember even one little yes. That's where practice comes in. The more you practice your yes, the easier it is. Yes connects us to Love, the only antidote to fear. Fear is a crypt that wants to entomb us in our no's. Love awakens us and brings us back to the life-giving yes that will save not only our own lives, but also ripple out Love to all the lives around us. These ripples of yes emanate in beautiful concentric circles of joy and affirmation until they meet all the other ripples of yes and form a beautiful ocean of Love. This is the daily practice of yes that can transform not only our own lives but also the lives of everyone, everywhere.

Are you ready to live in this world of yes?

If so, it's pretty darn simple.

Here is your practice: just say yes.

13

THE PRACTICE
OF COMPASSION/
NAMASTE

Missing the Mark

Growing up in a church that threw around a lot of words that landed big punches, words like *sin* and *evil* and *repentance*, I came into adulthood carrying a lot of religious baggage that I needed to shed in order to create any kind of meaningful spiritual practice. The word with which I struggled the most was *sin*. How I hated that word! Whenever I felt anything less than perfect, which was pretty much all the time, I struggled mightily not to tar and feather myself with that word. *Sin. Sin. Sin.* Sinning was never far from my thoughts. To be honest, I felt like a sinner more often than not. And so, at some point, I just gave up and thought, *Well, fine, then. I'm a sinner. So what?*

That worked okay when things were going well. But when I felt scared or anxious or ill, thinking of myself as a sinner made everything worse. Of course I deserved to suffer! I was a sinner! Yet as my spiritual practice became more important, something told me that I wasn't doing myself any favors with this thinking. That's why I'll never ever forget the gut-level relief I experienced the day I learned that the word *sin* was an archery term meaning "to miss the mark."

An archery term? How on earth had an archery term come to be so scary for so many of us for so many centuries? Well, fear, of course. When we believe we are inherently bad and unworthy of being saved by Love, fear has us right where it wants us. When I understood that, I knew I had to reclaim the word *sin* for myself. So, I asked myself, where was I missing the mark?

The answer was surprisingly simple, and it's true for us all: we miss the mark whenever we believe we can ever leave the Field of Love.

If archers miss the mark, they don't throw down their bows and give up, believing they are "bad," undeserving of ever trying again. What they do is practice.

That's why heart-centered Love practice is so transformative. Instead of trying to fix a deep-seated belief in inherent unworthiness, as manifested by lack of money or health or connection, we simply show up and practice Love every day. When we do, we remember our True Selves and feel our presence in the Field of Love. Then we are no longer missing the mark.

The fear-based teachings that we received are what cause us to miss the mark and forget the essential reality that is the Field of Love. As a result, we live our lives as though we're separated from each other and from Love. But we aren't—because we aren't isolated entities circling around in bubbles of fear. We always have and always will live as one in Love.

Becoming Love practitioners returns us to the grace of this beautiful truth. When we begin to feel the presence of Love, we wake up to the realization that there is only one thing any of us are really here to do: live as if none of us are or ever can be separated from Love. When we live like this, our experience of ourselves, of each other, and of our world changes. This is because when we choose Love, we act less out of fear and begin to see everyone as an equally beautiful expression of Love. We are living Love.

More than ever, this is what our world needs right now. *Living Love is not optional!*

The fact is, sooner or later, one way or another, the presence of Love will make itself felt in all our lives. Ultimately, Love is the only reality, and we are already Love practitioners. It's just that, all too often, fear cons us into forgetting our True Selves, and we move through the world acting out fear's screenplays.

Increasingly, studies reveal that human beings are more addicted, angry, lonely, isolated, afraid, divisive, violent, obese, and medicated than ever before in history. Because of this, we are seeking spiritual answers. Yet sometimes we worry that it's too late for ourselves, for our children, and for our planet.

That can make us feel too hopeless to believe that change is even possible. This is simply not true! Nothing is impossible to Love.

As Albert Einstein recognized:

"A human being is a part of the whole, called by us 'Universe.' Yet one experiences oneself as something separated from the rest—a kind of optical delusion of one's consciousness. . . . Our task must be to free ourselves from this prison by widening our circle of compassion to embrace all living creatures and the whole of nature in its beauty."

The whole human "problem" boils down to this: we have seen our little individual life and other people's little lives as problems to be solved and life as a problem-solving journey. We go through our lives afraid of what we see and try to fix it. When we do, we lock ourselves into the illusion of separation from each other and from our planet. By practicing Love, we shift all that. We free ourselves from the solitary confinement of our false separate selves and invite Love in to widen our circle of compassion.

More than ever, we all need to wake up to Love, to practice Love, and to live as what our True Selves know is true: each and every single one of us was, is, and always will be Love.

So, my dear friends, are you ready to live Love?

YOUR PRACTICE OF NAMASTE (OR COMPASSION)

If your answer is yes, then you're ready for our final practice together.

Together.

Meaning it cannot be done alone.

We have to do this together.

Namaste is a Sanskrit word that is thrown around a lot these days. It means many things, the most literal of which is "I bow to you." In Hindu practices, including yoga, it signifies a kind of holy adoration: "The divine in me sees and honors the divine in you." So when you see two people put their hands together and bow slightly while saying *namaste*, this is what it means.

I love this! The Love in one person is seeing and honoring the Love in another. This is the ultimate heart-centered Love practice. Because to practice this fully and deeply and authentically, we call upon all our other Love practices.

In order to see and honor the Love in another person, we have to first learn to see and honor the Love in ourselves.

We shift out of the problem-solving mind-set by learning to practice our heart-centered intentions.

We practice the pure and simple delight in being alive that we can only feel in Love.

We learn how to look through Love's dual lenses of gratitude and forgiveness in order to choose Love over fear.

We begin to witness our own thoughts with less judgment. When we do, we see others with less judgment.

We get to practice discernment every day, pulling out the weeds and leaving only the flowers.

We practice awareness by turning our *should* into good.

We say yes to Love, even as we honor our no.

We learn to be present right where we are by paying attention, being astonished, and telling each other about it.

We become willing to let go every day of everything by centering in Love.

And then from the hearts of our True Selves, rooted and grounded in Love, we take that into our lives, out to the wide world of "strangers," and we adore ourselves and everyone we meet. We can do this because we now know what it feels like to be adored. We have felt what it is to be adored in, by, as, through Love. From that place of adoration, we bow to each other as the divine Love in us sees the divine Love in them. And together, with our whole hearts, we say *namaste*.

ACKNOWLEDGMENTS

This book was inspired by—and is dedicated to—
the people and animals in my life who taught me
the meaning of Love by living Love.

We live Love by practicing Love.
By practicing Love, we live Love.

We live Love, because we are Love.
And Love only knows how to do one thing:
Love loves us all whole.
This is how Love heals.

Love always heals, because Love is all there is.
All we ever need is Love.

With special thanks to Jennifer Feldman,
Karen Osit, and Fiona Hallowell
for shepherding this book into being.

ABOUT THE AUTHOR

Victoria Price is the author of the critically acclaimed *Vincent Price: A Daughter's Biography* and *The Way of Being Lost: A Road Trip to My Truest Self*. She is a popular inspirational speaker on topics ranging from the daily practice of joy, living your legacy of yes, facing your fears and transforming your life through love-based practices, and making peace with your past stories to expand your creative futures. Price has appeared on *Good Morning America* and NPR's *Fresh Air* and *Morning Edition*, and her work has been featured in *USA Today*, *People*, *Travel & Leisure*, *Art & Auction*, and *The New York Times*. Her website is www.victoriaprice.com.